ACKNOWLEDGEMENTS

*T*o Brad and Bryce, my sons: Because you have forever changed my life – I love you and am thankful you trusted Dad and I to be your parents!

I am so grateful to my brother, Mike Grahek, and my mom, Jean Grahek, who always "have my back" and are a source of continued guidance and strength.

I am also grateful to my other family members and friends who have laughed and cried with me. A special "shout out" goes to my YaYa's (Chris Cowan, Shaunda Davis, Linda Holowati, Jane Vanderburgh, Joli Parks, Shari Jones, Susan Balisteri) & Colleen Pugh, Lisa McAlister, Erin Grahek and Michelle Gonzalez.

Collaborating with you, Chris Fadden, was such a remarkable experience. You're an amazing writer and friend. Blessings to you!

To the community of Union, Oregon: You surrounded our family with such compassion and care – I will never forget you.

Thanks to my work colleagues, especially Chris Mellett, Tom Queen & John Quintal – you always knew the right time to connect with me. Thanks for checking in and making sure I was doing OK.

A very special gratitude to my Opperman Family for your love, strength and grace.

To Normina for your wise counsel and coaching.

And finally to Sean - my kind, smart, empathetic, understanding husband; you opened my heart. There are no words to express how I feel about you, so "I love you" will have to do.

DEDICATION

To Dave, you are always with me.

ISBN: 1547228431
ISBN 13: 9781547228430

Take care of Yourself!

Melissa

FILLED WITH GOLD

A Widow's Story

Melissa Grahek Pierce
with
Christine Fadden

PREFACE

Words I associate with my first day as a parent: pizza party, Buddy the dog, Trix cereal, and shock.

It was an uncharacteristically sunny Sunday in Portland, Oregon and my husband Dave and I had just met the two young boys we were hoping to adopt. Brad, the older boy, was seven—a blonde kid who had already lost a few of his baby teeth, and was full of energy. Bryce, who had just turned five, was seemingly fragile, and followed every move his older brother made—literally. Together, Brad and Bryce had lived back and forth for five years between their birth mother, their paternal grandmother, and with several foster families—meaning, Bryce had not had a steady home since birth.

The idea was that we would be pulling these boys out of the foster care cycle and into their forever home. The idea also was that we would have at least three weeks to prepare for them.

Leave it to Buddy, our big goofy black lab, to speed things up.

Dave and I had been married for five years, but had known each other eleven years prior. We were best friends and we wanted children, but we couldn't conceive. Adoption made sense to us—I was nearing forty and Dave had just turned forty-one. Neither of us had been "baby crazy" to begin with, and so, we began to research our options.

The organizations that arranged adoptions for orphaned children in developing nations tugged at our heartstrings, but frankly, money was a concern. Wouldn't we rather save that kind of money *for our adopted children*? Adoption is a complicated process, whether you choose to look internationally or locally, but once we began to look at the state system, it made sense to us. Not only did it make sense, the number of children in the system was crushing. We began to pour through loads of overstuffed three-ring binders—looking at the faces and descriptions and personal anecdotes of Oregon's "lost," or "unwanted," or "neglected" children. There were so many. You wish you could adopt them all, but there are those you are especially drawn to.

Brad and Bryce's caseworker had written in his file: "Bryce stated that all he wants is '… a mom and a dad and a dog to lick his face.'"

And so there we were: We had driven from our home in Aloha that sunny Sunday morning in late February to the boys' foster home in Southeast Portland. We met their foster parents and got invited to accompany them all to the ultimate kids' birthday party spot: Chuck E. Cheese's. Between playing video games, wiping strings of greasy cheese off our chins, opening presents, volleying loose balloons, and stuffing ourselves with cake, Dave told Brad and Bryce we had a dog at home.

"His name is Buddy, and he loves kids!"

The boys were curious. Brad asked, "Can we go see him?"

What were their foster and potential adoptive parents to do? We asked the boys' foster parents if they could come home with us for a few hours—to meet our big goofy black lab. They said, "Sure, why not?"

Once at our house, the boys wanted to stay and Dave and I knew the boys would never leave. They were home, and our home would forever be fuller. We would be forever fuller.

This is what you believe—good and right and hopeful things last forever.

That evening, however, our cupboards were bare! While Dave and the boys played with Buddy, I shifted into business mode. I didn't have one second to look in the mirror and say to myself, face aglow and smile dreamy, "I'm a mom! Today, I'm a mom and Dave's a dad. We'll be hearing those words now—'Hey, Mom. Hey, Dad!' We'll hear the soft pitter-patter of feet in the morning and the—"

No! I didn't have time for the emotion of it all. This sudden parenthood felt practical. It didn't feel quite real yet and besides, with the kind of energy Brad and Bryce had, I doubted I would hear the soft pitter-patter of anything in the house ever.

The sparkly, glowy, shiny day would come. The signing of the papers and the official celebration would come, but first I had to figure out what we needed in the house to get us through the next twelve hours. Brad and Bryce would have to sleep in their clothes that night, and we would figure out a way to get them to school the next day, but they needed toothbrushes! They needed fruit and vegetables and peanut butter and jelly—okay wait—I knew what kids ate! But when my mom called and asked, "Hey, how'd your visit with the boys go today?" I laughed.

"Mom, they're staying. As in, they aren't going back to foster care. As in, I think they're ours for good!" And I hung up, went to the store, and bought a huge box of Trix cereal.

⚓

It isn't true that Dave and I were totally unprepared for the boys that night. Our search for children had begun several months prior and we had gone through all the legal and systemic steps for creating a family. We had purchased a few essentials. We had a booster seat and a car seat. We had bunk beds and the bare bones of a kids' room set up, because of a pre-Brad-and-Bryce story that was so discouraging it almost stopped us in our adoptive tracks. A few months prior to finding Brad and Bryce, we had been sure we would be bringing home three siblings from the Oregon foster care system.

Yes, after months of training, certification and a home study we were identified as a match for a sibling group of three, we were so sure the match was right, told everyone: "This is it! It's happening. Our dream is coming true. Our kids will play with your kids."

We told our parents: "You're getting three more grandkids."

We had envisioned ourselves suddenly a family of five, okay, a family of six, with Buddy.

We knew from the pages we had read in one of those thick, heavy three-ring binders who this lost trio would be when they entered our lives, and we imagined who they would become. Dave and I talked too, about who we would become—how we would learn and grow, as we taught and raised these strangers. And then the bottom fell out, there was a "glitch in the system," and our hearts exploded with a new and twisted ache of remaining childless.

The day we went to meet Brad and Bryce, we told hardly a soul. Not because we didn't want these two boys just as much as we had wanted the "lost trio," but because we wanted them even more.

Too many of our friends and family—so excited for Dave and I to share our awesome home and love and life with kids in need—had been hurt by the glitch in the system. We were being cautious, and that of course is when nature took over. BAM! Overnight, we became a mom and a dad. And we had a dog, a dog that didn't like to lick faces, but who was more than enough of a loyal and loving beast for two boys who knew more about loss and change than most adults did.

❧

It's hard to recall all the details of our first night with the boys. It was a whirlwind of shock, joy, getting shit done, and exhaustion. From that very first night, I knew though, parenthood was a task I could never have taken on without Dave. It became immediately clear that single mothers are Wonder Women.

In those first few months with the boys, I would sometimes panic when Dave wasn't around, assuring me, as he always did, "It's all going to be okay. It'll all work out."

But how will I get the boys from Point A to Point B in the car without having to turn around to stop them from fighting every five seconds?

Dave was a teacher; he was confident around "all things kid." I worried I might damage these kids more than they already had been.

Whatever had happened to Brad and Bryce prior to coming into our lives, Dave and I preferred not to know. With most state adoptions, you get the "basic notes" and beyond that, you can assume the worst. You assume that if the children you are taking in were not beaten or molested, they were neglected—which is in many ways, even worse.

When you choose to adopt, people warn you; they give you advice. *There will be challenges.* Brad and Bryce's biological family was torn apart. Nobody goes unscathed. At times, Dave and I could see how the love and shelter and security we provided was so foreign to the boys, that the only way they could absorb it, was to first reject it and respond to it with rage—especially Brad, who had seen more in his seven years in the system than little Bryce had.

Yes, the honeymoon would end. The haze of the "happy family" would lift from time to time and the past would seep in—no, it would explode things.

The third or fourth night into parenthood though, I remember Dave and I tucking Brad into bed and how this boy—this older and protective brother to Bryce, this frightened underweight bewildered seven-year old kid—said to us: "Are we safe in this house?"

"You have Buddy," we assured him. "We have an alarm system. You have us." And still, Brad always wanted to watch us lock all the doors and windows.

For three good years, Brad and Bryce had Buddy, until he died of old age, in 2008.

For five good years, the boys had a solid home, with an alarm system—and they had us.

Then one night, Dave died. He died suddenly, in bed, of what we will never know for sure.

This is the story of how Brad and Bryce and I made our way after losing the best man any of us knew—not a saint, not a God—but a guy that loved coaching sports year-round and fishing with his family & good friends, a dedicated teacher, a devoted husband, and an amazing father.

CHAPTER ONE

C hildren weren't alien to us. Dave and I had both hit either side of forty. We had been with our friends and siblings through the wondrous and wild births of their children. We had experienced festive first-year birthday parties and messy first-year birthday cakes, as well as fifth-year birthday parties—the kind that tire out the adults even more than the kids. And of course, we were surrounded by children every holiday. Children helped make the holidays!

Dave and I took our roles as aunt and uncle—by blood or by friendship—seriously, by being extra silly. We played with other people's kids, pushed them in strollers and swings, and listened to terribly cloying songs tinkling out of bright indestructible toys a thousand times because that's what you do with children. You watch *Barney* or *SpongeBob Squarepants* on TV.

You nurse boo-boos real and imagined.

And yes, we were probably *that childless aunt and uncle*, you know, the ones that wink and say, "Oh, let's break the rules a little today, kids." We'd buy the second scoop of ice cream, or the glittery lip gloss, or the noisy drum set —nothing of course that would set anyone off—nothing extravagant— but those small treats, like a box of that sugared cereal that tears up the roof of your mouth if you eat more than one bowl in one sitting.

We played and shopped and coached, we listened and counseled and cooed, and then, always, we parted—just the two of us. So no, children weren't alien to us, not by a long shot—but as much as we loved the children in our lives, they weren't ours. We didn't get to bring them home every night, tuck them into their beds with a good book, and bear primary responsibility for them for most of the rest of their lives.

We wanted that responsibility. We longed for it.

When it became clear that biology was not going to co-operate with our longings, Dave and I began to talk about adopting. We talked about what friends we both knew had been through, either as adopted children, or as adoptive parents. We decided we would be clear with the children we brought into our lives about their birth family and help them maintain healthy connections to their birth parents and siblings, if possible. We didn't want them to wonder, as a friend of mine always had, why they had been "given up."

The first adoption symposiums we went to were held in Portland, one at the Good Samaritan Hospital and another huge one, at the DoubleTree Hotel near Lloyd Center. The events were slightly overwhelming, or rather, the notion that so many organizations had so many children who needed loving homes was overwhelming. It was all slightly surreal.

Dave and I wandered from table to table. We asked questions; we answered questions. We picked up pamphlets— pamphlets about international adoption law and financing, and of course, pamphlets full of children. We were considering adopting children from Sierra Leone. The number of children orphaned there due to the ongoing civil war and HIV crisis was crushing. We had also talked about refinancing our house in order to make the process go as smoothly as possible. But then we wandered over to the Boys and Girls Aid Society booth, which works with Oregon state adoptions. We grabbed a few pamphlets from their table, and that is when things got real.

Some of the kids in the Oregon state system were unwanted, some were unloved, and some were orphaned, by death or by drugs or by just plain difficult circumstances. Some were six years old and some were sixteen; some smiled solo into the camera, and some, the photographer captured hugging and holding their siblings. The older they were and the more of them there were—these sibling teams—the harder they were to place.

All of the kids in the pamphlets, and all of the kids in the many three-ring binders we would be allowed to browse after we went through DHS training, came with mini-biographies. And all of the words in all of those biographies, we knew even before we began to talk "reality" with social workers, had been so carefully chosen.

Most of the children in the DHS foster care system, whether they'd been given up at birth or at age ten, would live, no matter what, with *some* of the effects of *some* of the words that had been suppressed on the pages that had been written expressly to bond them to a reader.

We knew this. We had read and done research. We had heard many stories of adoption: the good, the bad, and the ugly. But we weren't deterred by the idea there would be challenges. We would gamble; we would place our bets *against* the left-out elements of the stories we had read.

Dave and I were a great team. We would be great parents to kids who had, through no fault of their own, been left out of a support system many of us take for granted—family.

Dave and I wanted the unwanted. We had a lot of love to give.

Under each photo, we read: "Tony loves math!" or "Emily's favorite foods are spaghetti and pizza," or "Jonas is shy until he gets to know you." Each face held a mystery. You take these pamphlets home with you and thumb through them, side-by-side, silently. You pause. You breathe, but you aren't sure you can catch your breath. There are so many children.

You try to read between the lines, in the eyes of these children. You understand that each photo and summary of each child is constructed like a well-designed book cover. You close your eyes that night—or those many nights you are going through the process of choosing who you might have the honor of parenting—and you are on the floor of the New York City Public Library, a place you've never actually been, and you are looking up at a bookshelf—a very long, high, deep bookshelf.

Which "cover" will draw you to it?

Which story will you one day wake up to find yourself a part of? How will the children you choose to adopt change your life and the way you see the world—how will they change you and the way you see yourself?

I thought I knew myself fairly well back then.

⋯

Dave and I attended trainings, did our background checks and turned in our fingerprints. We handed in the photo album the DHS requests of all potential adoptive parents. We had thrown in photos of Dave and I camping, fishing, and playing in the snow. Our family and friends were included in this photo album—our nieces and nephews. We wrote essays addressing the question: "What kind of mother or father will you be?" We completed questionnaires: *Do you believe in spanking as a disciplinary method?* We both checked a big "NO" on that one.

Dave and I felt like we were in the PhD for Parents fast-track program—at Yale!—even before we ended up becoming parents overnight. We liked this program though. We had studied hard and we were a team.

Still, all the state-mandated self-explaining we were forced to do did lead to self-exploration and discovery. When Dave and I peeked at each other's questionnaire answers, or when we discussed certain aspects of our paperwork with our social worker, Erica, we sometimes surprised ourselves. In the process of writing out how we planned to parent, naturally, we examined how we had been parented. This conscious look back at my own childhood made me feel my dad's death acutely. It had only been one year.

Dave being there for me when my father was dying had brought us closer. Preparing for this next huge step in our lives—parenthood—bonded us even tighter. I'm sure this is true for most couples entering into parenthood and I definitely expected parenthood to change us, for the better and wiser eventually, but the adoption process forces conversations you might not even realize you might want to have before having children. It forces you to confront and address assumptions.

Most people who have kids the "natural" way might not necessarily dig into the questions Dave and I had to dig into: How am I going to parent? What have I learned from my parents and their parenting style? How do I handle stress? What was the biggest disappointment/loss in your life and how did you handle it? Which parent were you closest to during your formative years and why? What is the most difficult aspect of your marriage and how do you handle it?

This portion of the adoption process opened up a valuable dialogue between Dave and I, and after we had finished and received our "stamp of approval" from the DHS, we realized how much better off all children might be if every prospective parent had to sit with these questions and think things through. We have all seen "those parents" out in public, the ones that make us wonder why parenthood doesn't require a test, or an interview, or a license.

Parenting is far more practical stuff than fluffy stuff. Yes, I imagine that especially when you are bringing your biological child into the world, there is an aura of idyllic romance—the little being that is half you, half him has "taken root" and is on the way. But when Dave and I realized we would never be able to conceive biologically, we accepted the cards we'd been dealt, felt bad and grieved briefly, and then we moved forward with our plans to make a family.

Fast forward to the idea of adoption, and then to adopting not one child, not one *baby*, but a set of older, harder-to-place children.

Fast forward to bringing Brad and Bryce home to meet Buddy.

From the time it took to drive from Chuck E. Cheese's to our house, we had become the parents of two boys—two ravenous, anxious, loving, eager, smart, energetic fully formed human beings.

⚔

The person who had written Brad's description—Donna, the boys' caseworker—had labeled him "sporty" and Bryce, "artistic and creative." Because Dave coached football, basketball, and baseball, we assumed Brad would gravitate toward him, and Bryce toward me. That first evening they had come home with us, when we realized we had nothing to prepare for dinner, we had taken the boys to Dairy Queen.

Sitting there eating ice cream, Brad saw the little plastic box—the kind people drop quarters and dimes, and sometimes, a dollar bill into.

"Look at all that money! It's for kids who need help," Brad said. He looked at us. "We're kids. We need help!"

And with that, Bryce started to cry.

Dave looked at me across the table—I'll never forget it—with a "What do we do?" expression on his face. Maybe it was at that exact moment, that confusing and pivotal moment, where he and I realized the gravity of the situation. Bryce was five years old, and probably totally overwhelmed. These kids were hurt, scared, lonely, and tired.

Dave mouthed to me, "Hug him?"

So I did. I scooped up tiny underweight Bryce, and I melted. We weren't going to fill these boys with Dairy Queen every night, that was for sure, but we were going to feed these kids better. Whoever bonded more in those first few months—it didn't matter, as long as there was bonding.

So, that was our first lesson in parenting: Expect that all your expectations will be turned upside down. Brad wanted to hang out with me more, and Bryce was drawn to Dave's male energy. Before his death, Michael, the boys' biological father, had his share of struggles. He moved in and out of the boys' lives, so neither of them had really spent that much time with him. Actually, Bryce doesn't remember his dad. But some absences and needs, you don't analyze. You don't have time.

There would be plenty more surprises, good and not so good. Brad would not always want to hang out with me, of course, and he and I would face some severe challenges, even early on, but in those first few months, we tucked them in at night—assuring them, "Yes, all the doors and windows are locked. Yes, you are safe here. Yes, you *both* are staying. You won't be separated."

The boys' older brother, Brandon, was in another foster care home, but immediately we were open with him and he has been part of our family since Brad and Bryce moved in. Our second Christmas together, in fact, we packed the three boys into our car and drove to Salem, where their sister Brittany was in juvenile lock-up. She had made coloring books for Brad and Bryce. She was so excited to see her brothers, and she was kind to us—we spent that Christmas Day in the cafeteria, surrounded by barbed wire fences and guards, playing board games and laughing. Having basically raised themselves, Brittany and her brothers are all very tight.

Brad and Bryce knew we were technically "just" their foster parents. They didn't know the details, but we knew the adoption process might take awhile. Legally, their biological mother's parental rights had not been terminated. She was insisting on certain rights, so we would see her and the boys would too—as long as she was clean. She was a heroin addict, so there were times she was clean and times she wasn't. We worried, of course: What if we pull up to our meeting spot and see that she has marks on her arms? How will it affect the boys if she's totally wacked out and we have to drive away?

Fortunately for Brad and Bryce, it never turned out that way. Shanna, their birth mother, took the visits very seriously and was always respectful of our roles. Dave and I would stand at the sidelines of the park, while the boys spent time with her, and over time, we came to learn that yes, of course, sometimes people struggle to parent. Shanna loves her children, she was just unable to take care of them.

During these early days and months, I would fear against all logic that Shanna would come to our house and kidnap her boys back. At first, I thought she was a monster, but I came to feel for her. Addiction can overtake anyone—it's a disease, not a sign of weakness. Eventually, I hoped she could find peace and contentment in the fact her boys would be well taken care of. But yes, I have to admit that in those early days and months, fear and protective urges weighed on my mind in a way they didn't weigh on Dave's. Maybe it was because he didn't have to deal with his counterpart—the boys' father, Michael, had died.

"Maybe," I said to Dave, "It's some kind of mother-to-mother thing getting under my skin. How would you feel if you had to face the man who had neglected his children—not fed them at times? Bryce is five years old and still in diapers. The system failed them, yes, but first, his mom and dad did."

When I worded it that way, Dave understood. It took me time to warm up to Shanna, but as with most everything in life, my fears were worse than reality. Shanna had never been anything but cooperative. She always did her best.

But men really do have it good—whereas I was often emotional and sometimes insecure about my role as a mother, Dave had an almost instant paternal confidence. We'd both had great childhoods and loving parents, but me, I was still devouring all the parenting books I could. I was observing all the other mothers like a hawk. I was never sure I was packing the right juice boxes in the boys' lunches or for a soccer game.

Should I tell Brad and Bryce to settle down when they do this or that, or is that helicoptering?

I wasn't a basket case or anything. I had always been a natural when it came to handling emergencies, but this wasn't an emergency, exactly. Sure, we were all in therapy at the time. We all needed support, even Dave, for some of the deeper darker issues even he, with all his experience teaching and coaching kids, didn't quite know how to address.

Dave and I, along with the social workers and therapists, we all knew that those elements that are never spelled out in the files potential adoptive parents see were buried deep in the boys. We decided early on to let any issues rise organically. We didn't make a big deal out of the times the boys visited with Shanna, Brandon, and Brittany. If Brad, being older but still only seven, wanted to tell us things, we would listen. *But he was only seven.* There were pre-trauma and even pre-verbal issues at work, and he had no way of talking his sadness and fear out—he could only rage. We could only let him. We could only give school counselors and teachers a heads up when the boys were coming off a visit from their mom. We were learning every single day, at times, about triggers—about what seeing birth parents can trigger.

We learned too, that the boys' social worker, a wonderful woman named Donna, was a trigger as well. Always professional and doing her job, she would come for her monthly welfare check-ins. Were our fire alarms working? Were our cupboards full? How were things going?

Those first few months, every time Donna knocked on the door, Brad would race to his room and hide under his bed.

Donna, after all, had removed him from his mother's home, and then from his grandmother's home, and then from various foster homes.

Of course Brad hid from Donna. Despite having Buddy and knowing there were two boxes of his favorite granola bars in the cupboard, despite our constant reassurance and the new sports equipment and the fact we loved his brother too, he thought we might let him go. And I had thought Bryce breaking down from exhaustion and exhilaration at Dairy Queen our first night was heartbreaking.

Yes, we needed support with all that we didn't know and might never know about the boys, because there are ways in which all the unsaid things in those files you never look at again, show up.

They often blow up.

We decided to have Erica come to the house instead of Donna, and those in charge of such things approved it, but through it all, Dave and I had to be calm, cool, and collected for Brad and Bryce. Dave, again, mostly was. I, again, mostly had to train myself to be chill—for the first time in my life.

I had to show both boys that all the cupboards were constantly full, and to assure them they would never run empty. Even when Brad, at seven, destroyed his bedroom in a fit of rage—breaking a television, amongst other things—I had to assure him he could stay—he was home. When he had those fits, and my first instinct was to not allow a child of seven to throw a tantrum and break things, it took the support of a team beyond the team Dave and I were.

We were learning a lot.

"What's that book, Mom?" Brad once asked me. "The Exploding Child?"

The Explosive Child, which is a brilliant book about attachment disorder, was my Bible. *Twenty Things Adopted Kids Want Their Parents to Know* was my life raft. Dave was my rock.

⚒︎

Dave sort of remembered the first time we met. I was one of his sister's good friends. Nina and I were both getting our paralegal certificates, and she had invited a few girlfriends to go watch her brother play with his band. Dave played bass.

Our friend Sheila, tall and blonde and wearing a mini-skirt that night, caught Dave's attention. I remember it vividly—it's the thing you love and hate about having stunning friends. Or, more specifically, it's the thing you love and hate about having friends who have long legs. You walk into a room and watch men's eyes dart like magnets. You adjust your bra and hope there are a few boob men in the crowd.

There always are.

But we were mostly there for a girls' night out—girls, uninterrupted thank you very much.

Dave and his band—at the time, he was in a band called Funk n'Judy—played originals and covers that night, at the Melody Ballroom in Portland. They played one of my all-time favorites, *Brick House.* It was one of those nights you would try to leave the dance floor for a quick break, but another funky song would start up and draw you back in.

I hold Nina responsible for everything that happened between Dave and I after that night. She set Dave and I up as roommates. True, we were both looking. And though finding a place in Portland back in the Nineties was no where near as hard or expensive as it is now, it is always nice to count on a friend's word that someone you'll share a kitchen and bathroom with is a decent human being and not a slob, or a serial killer.

But actually, Nina never did tell me Dave *wasn't* a serial killer. What had I done?

That first night Dave and I were official roommates, I laid there in my bed wondering, "Who the hell is this guy and what have I signed up for?"

I listened for signs he was asleep—did he snore? No snoring. I listened for sounds outside my door. Was he out there in the hallway? Was he naked? In the kitchen? What was I doing sharing living space with somehow I didn't know?

The later it got, the wilder my imagination became. Nina was a great friend and she still is, but does anyone ever really know anyone—*even their own family members?* How long was our lease? Why hadn't I just found a cute little studio apartment? Oh no!

I got up and dragged a heavy chair across the floor and put it against the door. I knew I wasn't going to be able to sleep otherwise. Did Dave hear that and wonder, "What is wrong with this person I've just moved in with? Why does it sound like she's moving furniture at 2:00 a.m.? I hope she isn't this noisy every night."

I told Dave this later on, when we started dating. But even our first attempt at dating was, well, awkward.

It had turned out that we made ideal living partners. We became fast friends, talking late into the night, playing cards, and being okay with dating other people. Even as we were realizing we were attracted to one another, neither of us wanted to ruin such a good and rare thing—we made great roomies! And then one of those late night talks—it was a white and snowy night and Dave built a fire—we took a chance at ruining our good thing. We didn't exactly sleep in our own separate bedrooms that night. And Dave's *bed?* Well, it wasn't even a bed exactly—it was a twin foam mattress tossed on the floor. We chose my bedroom and my queen bed—it smelled nicer.

For about a week, we kissed. We hovered in this new state. We didn't celebrate it and we didn't analyze it, but when Dave said, "Let's keep it on the down low," and I said, "And not even tell Nina?" and he said, "Yeah," I said, "No way."

I called it off.

Dave was a private person. I had come to know that as his roommate, and I would respect that in him throughout all our years together. But early on, I was excited. Wasn't this great fun news to share with our friends? Hey, it's not like I was jumping the gun and asking him to announce we were likely to get married one day. I just wanted him to reach for my hand in public. C'mon!

That wasn't his deal though, so we went back to being roommates. There were no hard feelings. We continued to play cards and drink beer together. I fell into another relationship that lasted nine months, and Dave did his thing. He was a substitute teacher at the time, and he fought forest fires during the summer. He had no papers to grade, no meetings to attend, and he got a natural workout.

⊯⊱

It was inevitable, and everyone who knew us told us so when we finally coupled back up and shared the news: "We're dating!"

"Of course," everyone said. "You two were always meant to be together."

And then I moved out, so Dave and I could really date.

Shifting gears—again, and for real this time—was no big deal for us. We were friends first and foremost, and neither of us was a mushy romantic. Love is a many splendored thing and I believe in the power of love and love lifts us up where we belong—I'm not immune to all the big red hearts and Cupid shooting arrows magic, but Dave and I were low-key about our relationship. We continued to do what we always did: We talked and laughed; we got on each others nerves once in awhile; we pushed each other to think and to grow; and we spent time with our friends and families.

We did do too, a few things we hadn't done before. I tried to introduce Dave to wine tasting. Wine never became his thing—he was a beer drinker—but at least he gave it a shot. Dave introduced me, a city girl, to the great outdoors. We hiked, camped, and fished. We played in the snow and went inner-tubing. Dave and I played in the woods. We jumped into freezing cold lakes.

I guess I'm starting to sound like a romantic here. But it is romantic, I suppose, to fall in love with your best friend and to wake up every day to the kind of partner you can fully be yourself with. Dave and I rarely had to assess where we were as a couple once we started to date the second time, and once we declared it.

We just were.

We were happy sitting next to each other at home on the couch, and we were happy traveling abroad with our best friends.

We were happy in Thailand in August of 2000, when Dave departed from his non-romantic modus operandi, and got down on one knee to propose marriage.

Now, you might be picturing a southeast Asian sunset and the silhouette of two people walking slowly into it, holding hands. No one else is around and this couple has no responsibilities or cares in the world. The man drops to a knee...

Or no, wait: Maybe the couple is swinging in an oversized hammock beneath a few palm trees, sipping one oversized frothy pastel-colored cocktail from two straws. The man spills out of the hammock onto the sand, and gets on one knee…

No.

The truth is, Dave and I were vacationing in Thailand with a group of friends. We were all lounging on the beach drinking cheap beer and lazily watching the world go by, which on that beach that day meant watching tourists run to and fro in the surf, and smiling at, but not giving in to every woman walking by and hawking beautiful sarongs and trinkets for tourists.

My friends were in on Dave's plan. And despite the fact that he and I had discussed getting married, I was absolutely clueless.

At a certain point, after Joli and I had gotten pedicures and massages, someone called a Henna tattoo artist over to our little plot of shaded sand.

"Yes! Let's linger here a little longer and get our hands and feet painted," we all agreed.

Even the guys wanted tattoos. We were in bathing suits, t-shirts, and towels, laughing and taking photos of ourselves. This was years before Facebook and selfies. This was five years before Dave and I would adopt the boys.

Our hair was wet and sandy, our skin was warm. We had doused ourselves in so much *Skin so Soft*, the mosquitoes slid right off us. This was *not* years before the world knew about the importance of slathering on a strong sunscreen, but we didn't care. We were young, we were on vacation, and we were from Oregon. We wanted tans that would last at least part way through the rainy Pacific Northwest fall.

"Dave," I said, "What's your design look like?"

He had been keeping his body turned away from me while the woman painted his arm. Dave had good arms. He had fireman's arms.

"Just some squiggles," he said.

We all felt so chill. It was the year 2000—it was kind of magical. We'd seen our first century turn. We were living in post-Prince 1999 times. We were all in our thirties.

And then Dave turned to show me his tattoo. Inside a small hennaed heart were two words: MARRY ME.

It was the first time in my life that anyone had managed to pull such a huge surprise on me. How hadn't I noticed Dave giving Joli the signal to dash off to our hotel room and bring back the ring? How had everyone kept such straight faces?

My Thai tan didn't last until our wedding day, which took place four months later in Oregon. But Dave's impermanent tattoo, is a permanent lifetime souvenir.

CHAPTER TWO

O ur wedding took place on December 9, 2000. Both my mother and father walked me down the aisle, which was extra sweet because the year prior, Dad had suffered a stroke and his health had begun to decline.

Before we got married, Dave had become a full-time math teacher in Forest Grove. I got my paralegal certificate, and in 1998 found a full-time job at a financial services company, which was one of the most fortunate decisions I have ever made. Immediately, I knew I'd chosen the right line of work and the right employer. While I was there, I did everything I could to make the sales team's job easier—I prepared proposals, contracts, addendums, and commissions. A couple times a year, I would travel for business, and eat at restaurants I couldn't afford then, and can't afford now.

At Christmastime, the sales team and my boss, Dick, would knock it out of the park in terms of gifts they sent me. I took care of them and they took care of me. When

Dave and I moved to eastern Oregon, the company allowed me the flexibility to work from home. When Dave died, the team demonstrated even more generosity—giving me and the boys extra money and helping us set up a scholarship in Dave's name.

My first years at the company, while Dave and I lived in Aloha, a few female colleagues and I formed the *YaYas.* We are together still—taking glitter and glue guns to everything, and meeting up for cocktails to sing Karaoke until our throats are sore. Without my *YaYas,* my work crew, and boss, dealing with life after Dave's death would have been much harder. I of course had my family and friends and Dave's family and friends to grieve and heal with, but you can never underestimate how crucial it was for me not to have to deal with the added burden of wondering if I would lose my job.

━╬┼╾

The year after our wedding, Dave and I bought our first house, in Aloha, a suburb of Portland. We had been growing frustrated with the houses available in our price range—Portland has always been infamous for its housing prices being disproportionately high compared to salaries. But one day on my way home from work, I saw a man staking a "For Sale by Owner" sign in his front lawn and I pulled up and asked if I could see inside.

The place was perfect for us.

2001 was still the pre-cell phone era, so I sped home to Dave. With the help of a realtor friend, we made our first dream as a married couple come true. When the boys came to that home four years later, and shortly after that, a bigger home we purchased, the boys helped Dave build a deck, we all painted and landscaped and revamped that house so that it was completely ours.

For those first few years though, before the boys, even with our suburban existence and 40-hour a week jobs, Dave continued to play in bands around Portland, and his sister and our friends and I continued to put on our non-Mom jeans and drink beer and dance into the wee hours of the morn. Some of the crew had babies or young children at home, but we loved our city and our guys up there on stage hammering out tunes we could groove to. In your thirties, you can still pull late-ish nights and get your kids to school on time the next day. My friends were doing this. None of the couples in our circle was the kind who gave up their own life entirely to parent. Maybe this is true of most people of a certain era, or maybe our crew wasn't quite ready yet to leave our late twenties behind, I don't know. Either way, between working and contributing to society like mature adults, and playing hard, Dave and I began toying with the idea of starting a family of our own.

And then, we started trying. We stopped using birth control.

Over the months, for a few weeks at a time, we'd wait for my period *not* to come. We'd get ready for work every morning, Monday through Friday, not necessarily talking baby names, but buzzing with that unique taste of possibility. When you take the leap from doing everything you can to prevent pregnancy to going for it and hoping for it, something shifts on a cellular level. Maybe it's the animal in us, but knowing, "This month could be the month our DNA

21

latch together to make a new life," puts you in a different headspace, almost a spell. Would this month be the month? No. Okay, how about this month? No. Next month, maybe?

But for every month we tried—we had fun trying—my period always came.

During this time, I wondered, "What's wrong with me? What's wrong with my body?" I thought it had to be me, because as much as I hate to admit it, I had been careless about birth control a few times in my youth, and had never gotten pregnant.

Dave and I decided we would get tested, but he put his off—typical man, really. So when we went in to the clinic and the doctor looked at me and said, "It's not you," Dave bit the bullet and went in for his tests. We discovered his immune system was making antibodies that attached to his sperm, making it harder for them to swim along with low sperm count. The production of these antibodies could have been caused by an ancient injury to the testicles—but either way, we both felt disappointed and didn't talk about it much. I felt terrible for Dave, but oddly enough, I had somehow always known I would never conceive.

We then started to discuss alternate routes to parenthood.

In 2003, Dave and I were about to go down the fertility science tunnel, and then my father was diagnosed with a brain tumor.

You do put aside the notion of making a new life when the life of the man who made you is going to end.

When Dad got sick, fortunately, my siblings and I all lived close by. We took turns staying at our parents' home and helping our mother. Dick graciously let me work from their house a few days a week. Sad, stressed, and exhausted, the animal in us knows: "Now is not the time to procreate." Hell, even if my body had suddenly been able, my heart wouldn't have been in it if either Dave or I had wanted to try. Dave and I didn't want to try. We stopped trying.

※

My father, Leo, survived colon cancer when I was fourteen, so I guess it was always in the back of my head that he would die one day. I mean, we all will—but I probably lived with a semi-heightened always-present awareness that my dad, as big a provider and personality as he was, was also fragile.

Dad smoked and partied, ate rich food, and started having a series of small strokes in the mid-Nineties. The strokes slowed him down, but then a big one hit in 1999. We all thought that would be the end right there and then, but we would have four more years together.

For a spell, my father lost his ability to speak and walk. In the rehabilitation center we took him to, all he would do was constantly fold a washcloth. He would start to forget at this time who my mother was. He could remember me, my brothers, and all of his friends, but he once said to my brother, "Where'd Jean go? I haven't seen her in a long time." My mother, Jean, had just left the room.

He knew the Jean he had married—recognized her in old photographs—but the Jean caring for him now was becoming a stranger. You wonder if the mind protects itself from what would be an agonizing awareness of putting a life partner in the position of caretaker. Although, no, we all filled that role in my father's final years—some of us he recognized unfailingly until the end.

Of course, my mother was determined my father would walk and talk again, and thanks to her unwavering love for him and to the rehab staff, he did and he was able to come home. I don't know how long she might have held out hope his memory would heal too. I have never asked her. When he did gain his ability to speak and walk again, the problem then was that he would wander off. He wouldn't go far—he was physically incapable, but from 1999 on, my father could not be left alone. His memory never did return to full capacity.

Reversing roles and becoming parent to one of your parents is never easy or pretty, but I will always be grateful that when things took a turn for the worse in 2002, I got to spend a huge portion of my Dad's final six months in my parents' home. I am fortunate I was able to be there for my mom, when she was experiencing such pain over knowing time with her husband was drawing to a close, and her husband no longer knew who she was. She handled it all with such grace, and I continued to learn from my parents what it means to promise another human being that you will be with them in sickness and in health.

I was so grateful my father had lived to watch me exchange vows with Dave.

Dave, who my father had always liked, was by my side during my father's decline. Dave was in fact, the Hero of New Years Eve 2002—when the shit hit the fan. Dad disappeared that day, when Mom had slipped out of the house for five minutes. You know how urgent things pop up last minute; she probably had to buy a dozen eggs. But when the alert was sent out: Leo is missing!—Dave and I hopped in the car to scour the streets of King City near their home. Everyone, including the police, got involved.

And then my brother Mike said, "Maybe he went to his old office."

Dad's old office was in downtown Portland, and although the building was still there, his office had long ago closed shop. My father had been a salesman for Conrail Railroad. He sold space on rail cars, wearing a suit and polished shoes to work every day. He loved his job; he loved trains. He and I took a father-daughter trip once on Amtrak, going all the way from Portland to Minneapolis. And although I wasn't twenty-one at the time, he bought me a *California Cooler.* For anyone unfortunate enough to know what a *California Cooler* tastes like, I'm sorry, but that was probably one of the best drinks I have ever had—because my father bought it for me.

Cheers, Dad, I have some of your railroad art in my house today and have graduated to real wine.

My brother was right though, the day our father went missing: Leo, the retired railroad man, in fact had made way to his "old office," but of course, had found another business in it's place. He went and had a cup of coffee in the deli of that building and began wandering downtown Portland, doing what we will never know, we guess that some kind soul helped get him on the right bus. I was on foot asking all the businesses near their home if they had seen my Dad. Dave, who was circling the neighborhood in our truck and becoming more and more desperate—*Oh, God, the Tualatin River*—saw my dad get off the Number 12 bus. He pulled a U-ey and helped my Dad get in. Dave told him that a lot of people were worried about him and looking for him. As Dave swept Dad back to my parents' condo, Dad was so proud of himself, laughing and smiling and although we were all furious and concerned, we were relieved. We all laughed a little bit too.

Around this time, in 2002, laughter from my father was not always predictable. He was becoming increasingly agitated, to the point where even with his beloved grand-kids, he would sometimes lose patience. When he went in for an MRI after having yet another stroke, doctors discov-ered what they had missed in prior rounds—a brain tumor. OHSU is one of the best medical facilities in the country, so we took him there, prepared to do whatever it took to win the fight against yet another injustice to Leo's head. But the prognosis was brutal: *There is nothing we can do to fix this. He has a couple months.*

Dad refused treatment anyway. "I don't want anybody knocking around in my head," Dad said.

The awareness I had lived since my teen years—which had always lurked far enough below the surface that it hard-ly affected me—emerged. It was time to start counting each day with my dad as a blessing—my dad who had never once failed to let me know he had my back.

With Dad dying, my family came together—taking turns living with my parents for 48-shifts and providing as much relief as we could to Mom. The hospice team too, was wonderful. As the end drew close, we were told we had about a week, but as it turned out, we had two days. We thought of course that we had prepared ourselves, but the hour my father drew his last breath came as a total shock. My mother and I sat on the bed with him, and Dave stood in the doorway.

My father died on July 16, 2003, one day after he had turned seventy-five.

———

Brad and Bryce would have loved my father in his pre-decline days, and he would have loved them. Knowing what I know now about raising two boys—two boys from the foster care system, or from your own body—is that the more amazing male role models they have in their lives, the luckier they are. The boys did and do have a lot of amazing men in their lives—Dave helped ensure this while he was living, and after he died. But knowing my dad would have been icing on the cake.

When Dave and I brought Brad and Bryce home that first night and I was on the phone with my mother, on the way to the grocery store and in full practical-Melissa mode, I wished my father could have been on the other end of the line too. There would be many moments— celebrating a birthday, or just gathering at my parents' house to eat pizza—when I'd miss him. When Dave died, I wanted my father. What would my father think of me today? What if today, I'm a stronger more fulfilled daughter than I was a decade ago?

You grieve: You go through the steps, you know you'll never see the person who has died again and you land, eventually, in a place of acceptance. But in every happy or triumphant moment, you want them back—if only to exchange a split second of a smile or a laugh or a high five. You never lose the feeling of wanting to provide for your parents moments of pride, and the sadness when you lose a

parent sometimes seems to exist less in what you are missing by them being gone, and more in all they miss out on.
I've got a son in college now, Dad, and let me tell you, this
was not always a given.

Right?

My father would have loved visiting us when the boys
were still young, before college was even a consideration, in
Eastern Oregon. Dave's parents had raised him in Eastern
Oregon, and we decided to move there because we had
spent so many summers on Wallowa Lake, and thought it
would be great to provide Brad and Bryce "a small town
upbringing."

We were able to leave the city life and the opportunities
it affords because Dave found a dream gig—he was hired as
a full-time music teacher. My boss, Dick, who had been fully
supportive while my father was dying and when Dave and
I had ended up parents a few weeks earlier than expected,
showed again—tremendous support. I would keep my job
and work remotely.

"Wow!" a few of my friends in Portland said. "You'll be
living the dream—working from home in your pajamas."

The pajama dream is *the* dream those who don't work
from home have. I had that same dream, for a short while.

With our jobs set and the prospect of life slowing down,
Dave and I began the search for a new home. The boys were
totally into it. The housing market was our only challenge.

In 2007, the housing bubble was, as everyone knows,
about to implode. We could not sell our house in Aloha, so
we rented it. Finding a home near Union, where Dave was
going to teach, proved harder than we expected too. Finally,
we found a great place located on six acres, on the side of

Mount Emily in La Grande, thirty minutes from his school. This was not a bad commute for Dave, but note to all future small-town-living work-from-home dreamers: When you look at mountain homes in the summer, in an area known for harsh winters, envision those homes under a few feet of snow. I'm not talking about the drag of a winter commute here; I am talking about winter silence and isolation.

We took the place though. I had an inkling it might be too remote, but witnessing the level of Dave and the boys' enthusiasm, well, I repressed my intuition and resolved to embrace my inner pioneer woman!

There was much to embrace about our life on Mount Emily, in all the seasons—this is true.

That first fall, Brad was in fifth grade and Bryce was in second. The boys would hop in the truck with Dave after breakfast, and head into Union, thirty minutes away. In addition to attending an excellent school where their father was teaching, they also had a four-day school week. Life on Mount Emily started out pretty sweet. We had a few neighbors who liked to keep to themselves, and we had total privacy. When the snow started to fall, Dave would take the boys out and drag them on a sled behind his four-wheeler. We did drink hot chocolate and build snowmen, shovel snow and have snowball fights. Norman Rockwell, had his ghost stumbled by, would no doubt have singled us out as a truly happy unit. Brad and Bryce wore the healthy glow of always being outdoors. On six acres, they could step outside and roam, climb, explore, and completely exhaust themselves.

When I think back to that first winter, and the snow falling, and all of us playing in it, I also think about how much wood Dave and Brad and even little Bryce chopped in preparation. Dave knew winters in Eastern Oregon. He knew mountains and forests and fires. We had a cozy home, warmed, as they say, three times over by the wood we burned. The boys had friends at school, and on our three-day weekends, we were a tight playful family up on the mountain. When Dave and the boys were with me, I couldn't have asked for more.

When they weren't with me though, it was hard. They might have been only thirty minutes away, but after that first winter, even when the first spring came and bees were buzzing and a step out the front door meant receiving a blast of pine-scented air friends who live in cities can only associate with camping—I was lonely as hell.

I missed working in an office. I missed my boss, Dick, my friends and my office mates. What I know now is this: Some of us thrive in an office setting, and it's nothing to be ashamed of. *The Office* is such a kickass TV show precisely because, as wacky and as tedious as office life can sometimes be, we are all in it together. In addition to watching sales grow or deals being made, or even making copies or analyzing data, whatever it is people in an office do, we also watch each others' kids grow. There's always Friday too, and the beautiful release of Happy Hour!

Working in my pajamas at home alone, which in truth I rarely did, was not satisfying. Before working from home, I clearly had no way of knowing what the challenges would be. Those challenges hit me fast. That little inner voice I'd suppressed in the summer when we purchased our home became a *big* inner voice—as in, a voice that wanted to scream. Okay, I wasn't hearing voices, but when I say I would feel a wave of excitement every time I had to go to the grocery store, I am not exaggerating.

Lo and behold, I was a person who needed people—even if those people were running five cans of soup over a scanner, asking me if I'd like paper or plastic, and taking my money.

Being a work-from-home mom in a small town where "politically" I was a bit of an outlier—I'm from Portland: I'm liberal—was challenging. Raising Brad and Bryce was challenging too. We were the Norman Rockwell family plenty of days and weeks and seasons up there, but the boys were also continuing the fight against their demons. Chopping wood and having friends, running with a dog and kabbobin in the woods cannot erase all that takes place—or that doesn't—in the formative years.

Dave and I knew going in that working through the boys' issues around attachment would take time, perhaps a very long time. Of course, I never imagined I would end up without Dave, alone to ride these issues out. But when he and the boys were off at school and I was home alone, I realized I had to wrangle a few of my own issues too—or first. Or soon. It was hard to express it then, and it still is, mainly now because Dave is gone, but up on that mountain, my soul was filling with resent. I felt sometimes like we were living out *The Shining*—filmed in Oregon, by the way.

Alone, I'd think of Jack Nicholson chopping through that hotel room door, delivering his famous line: "Wendy, I'm home!"

But no, wait: I never left home to return to it at the end of the day. I was home all the time and I hated it! So now what?

Years after Union and back in Portland, I now know the Melissa of today would never have agreed to move into a house on the side of a mountain away from civilization. I know I don't have to prove to myself I've got pioneer woman qualities or tastes. I don't. Had we lived in town amongst people —I probably would have been happier, but I was never fully at home in Eastern Oregon. It's a gorgeous region and we still travel and visit family and friends there— Eastern Oregon is the place that helped shape Dave into the man he was.

He and I did discuss what was happening to me there. Dave loved me and didn't want me feeling so isolated. We tried to sell the home several times, but couldn't. The U.S. housing market slump lasted a brutally long time. Finally, in the middle of the winter of 2010, we decided we would leave the Mount Emily home come hell or high water in June 2011, but Dave died there in January.

❦

A small town will come to your rescue in ways, as a city-dweller, you may never have the fortune (or misfortune) of experiencing. When Dave died, the town of Union would not only rescue me and the boys, but it would mourn with us too.

When we first moved to Eastern Oregon, Dave rallied with the Optimists' Club to start Union's own football team. Prior to this, Union's players had merged with La Grande's. With Dave and the army of fathers he recruited to help grow the team, Union would begin to beat La Grande, regularly. It was a rivalry our small town soaked up and reveled in.

I was alone four days a week working at home, but Union did feel like our town—our home—in many ways. Dave, especially, was loved. He was a private man, but when he did work in the public, he worked *for* the public. We were going to leave our Mount Emily home, but there was no doubt the boys would finish their years at Union High School.

In the meantime, with the boys' high school graduation far off, I had to deal with the issue of suddenly having become a person who cried at home alone a lot. I went and saw a therapist.

"I should be able to handle this," I would say. "I should be a stronger person. What's wrong with me? I need to fix myself, change myself, get better."

The therapist would say, "Just get out there and try to make new friends. Just pick yourself up and talk to people."

I saw him twice—what a dumbass! I knew myself well enough then to know I was not a shy person—in fact, that was the problem: I could have made friends with everyone in the grocery store within a week, but I had to work from home and I could not work that way.

Dave and I eventually made friends with other couples. Our kids bonded us instantly to the parents of other kids. We also joined the community choir, through Eastern Oregon University. The boys didn't sing—choir wasn't their style, but they would come down the mountain with us those evenings and play with kids whose parents also found joy in belting one out.

With choir, a creative outlet, I could reach a state of normalcy—that is, I cried less. Music had been Dave's life. Music is what brought us together. Music helped keep us together through the months I was beating myself up and

battling resentment. We had the family we had always wanted and we had great jobs. We were fortunate. What was
wrong with me? I just had to get through some boundary I
couldn't see yet.

In junior high and high school, I sang and performed
in choir. Singing has always felt good and has helped me
tune things out. In La Grande, I'd sing tears away. Back in
Portland years later, I'd grieve and sing tears out, and oddly,
the group I would sing with, knowing nothing about Dave
or his death, wouldn't bat an eyelash or miss a beat. People
who sing know its power to transform: Tears, I suppose, are
like tiny liquid keys to the next rooms we will inhabit.

Dave and I had a piano in our living room on Mount
Emily and we'd sing together. Little did I know then that
singing together releases oxytocin, a hormone responsible
for pair bonding and building trust. Oxytocin *is* harmoniz-
ing. It is released by both partners when they sing, or kiss,
or have sex. It is also released when a mother nurses her
baby—it flows both ways.

—❋—

Within days after Dave's death, the boys and I moved into
town. We were moved into town. Despite the shock and
grief, I felt safe. I knew the boys were safe. Our friends
opened their homes to them while I tried to take care of
business. The boys would finish the school year, and then, I
knew, we would move back to Portland.

Union is where Dave taught, where he was Mr. Opperman
and Coach Opperman. He came to the town in 2007 strictly
as a teacher, but when he saw the need for a football team,

he got people excited about it, and created one. The Union/ Cove football team kicked butt. In his role as band teacher, Dave instilled a requirement for all students: from 6th grade on every student had to learn how to play an instrument. He formed relationships with Eastern Oregon University that offered college music students internships for teaching music at Union schools, K-12.

Dave was never one to seek attention, but he got it because of who he was and what he did. When he saw a need—especially for youth—he became a mover, a shaker, and most importantly, a doer.

We were planning to leave our Mount Emily home and move into town in June of 2011 and in the fall of 2011, Dave was set to become the official Union High School football coach. He had taught a set of kids from a certain age—they all knew the same plays and held the same team philosophy—so it made sense for him to take the role. Dave and his friend and fellow teacher, Greg, were eyeballing the old school track as the perfect place to create new baseball fields. Dave coached Little League, and he and I were both on the county and city Little League boards.

When Dave died, the town was devastated.

Fittingly, because truly it was the only place the entire town could fit, his funeral service was held in the Union School gym. I was in no state to be aware of it, but hundreds of people attended. My besties from Portland—my YaYas—showed up, as did a crew from work (my company paid their way and their time off). The band played and the choir sang. I was aware of that. Two former university student-teachers came to lead and join them. Brad played the school fight song with the band on his trumpet.

We were moved into town by a parade of trucks. The women and men of Union dismantled and safely transported an entire 3000-square foot home of furniture, appliances, and things the boys and I had no energy to pack up, and brought us in closer to the center of things, where they could keep an eye out for us. There were people inside our Mount Emily house I had never seen before. I cried and cried as we left the house I had, for so long, wanted to leave.

The determination to make Dave's dream field a reality ripped through the town like one of the summer wildfires he used to fight when we first started dating. Every weekend a bunch of the most fantastic dudes dedicated their time to tracking down and obtaining donated materials. They built backstops. They graded the field. They put up chain link fence. Because they are men, I think, their grief went into that project. In every nail they hammered and every grass seed they spread down, they sought to keep Dave with them.

The Opperman Memorial Athletic Complex (OMAC) hosted its first Little League Opening Day Ceremony in May 2012. Everyone turned out from Union, and everyone came in to town—including Dave's parents and family. Everyone was joyous.

There is a memorial bench at the fields—our friend Darren had it made to honor Dave. You can't help but wonder, no matter what you believe about life, God, and where we go after death—does Dave sometimes sit there and watch the games he loved? Has he watched the kids he taught and coached grow up and win and lose on that field? Does he go back to our Mount Emily house and look for us, ever?

I know Dave is not lost. He wasn't in life and he wouldn't be in death. Whenever I got anxious about parenting Brad and Bryce—what's wrong with me, why am I so lame at this when all the other mothers seem so great?—Dave pulled me back to center. Nothing was wrong with me. Being a mother is the hardest thing you'll ever do. Being a father is too—but I still think men just give less of a shit about what other men or fathers think of them.

You wonder after death, because as many times as the question has been asked we still don't really have a sufficient answer for it, or at least I don't: Why does it take terrible, sad, devastating events to wake us up? To transform us? To push us past some truth we have been resisting, into a better version of ourselves? After Dave's death, several friends of ours got divorced. Were these events related? I was a pleaser when I said "yes" to the house on Mount Emily. I am not that woman anymore.

I could return to Union and sit on Dave's memorial bench for a month, and still not understand why and how suffering through crisis can lead us to the life path we most need to take. I am still, after singing and talking my way through my grief and the boys' grief, still, after falling in love and marrying another wonderful man, seeking answers.

CHAPTER THREE

"There is a sacredness in tears. They are not the mark of weakness, but of power. They speak more eloquently than ten thousand tongues. They are the messengers of overwhelming grief, of deep contrition, and of unspeakable love."

~Washington Irving, American writer

In all the years I was with Dave, I saw him cry just once. We were living in Portland. It was late spring 2006, and the boys were finishing up the school year—Bryce was in kindergarten and Brad was in third grade. We had hosted Dave's family a week or so prior for a Memorial Day weekend barbeque.

Deep asleep one night in early June, we were woken by Buddy. He was barking like crazy at whoever was knocking at the front door. I doubt we said a word, but I can bet we both were thinking, "Maybe if we just don't open that door, the bad news—whatever it is—won't find us."

The hallway between your bedroom and the front door presses in on you though, its walls already mimicking the heaving and constricting your flesh, your bones, and all your insides will experience, shortly—as soon as the initial shock begins to wear off and the first wave of sadness slams into you.

The police officer told us Dave's brother, Paul, had been in a car wreck. He had lost control, taking a corner too fast. The death had likely been quick.

"The" death, his death, Paul's death.

Dave and Paul had been super tight. They were fishing and camping buddies, and beer-drinking best friends. As the oldest of five siblings, Dave had always been a protector, even if he never would have called himself one. He was loyal. The only fisticuffs fight he had ever been in involved sticking up for his best friend in college. Other than that, Dave was known for being calm, cool, and collected. When other football coaches got in his face—which they did as soon as he started leading the Union boys to big wins—he'd piss them off even more by not engaging.

Dave could not protect Paul though. None of us can protect our loved ones from whatever it is that decides, "Bam! Today is the day—or the long stretch of months—I'll take this one from you."

After Dave's death, which would occur five years later—and suddenly just like his brother's had—I would learn from their sister, Nina, that she had found a medical record in Paul's belongings indicating that he either had a congenital heart condition, or trouble was developing. She had brought it up, too, she told me, trying possibly to urge her brothers to take better care of themselves. I don't know, I wasn't there, but either way, Paul had never followed up and Dave never did either.

It was nobody's fault, of course—teenagers aren't the only ones who think they're immortal. Dave had passed a physical exam with flying colors two months prior to his death, and because I opted out of an autopsy I will never be sure about the condition his heart was in. A psychic I would see later would tell me she saw a man pressing his heart— Dave—but his condition had seemed chronic to her.

Could have, should have, would have—again and again. What do you do? What do you believe? What do you tell yourself before you go to sleep at night?

What's the point? A bad heart, a strong heart, smoking and drinking, or being a teetotaler, taking a curve too fast in the middle of the night, thinking a little over-the-counter medicine will do the trick—the cause of death, particularly in sudden cases, seems worthless. Maybe we want to know the cause, only so we can answer more easily the question we will hear a hundred times: "How did he die?"

"Stroke, heart attack, an undetected tumor, a rare form of X, a car wreck. I. Don't. Know."

Nobody is comfortable with "I don't know."

So Paul died in a car wreck. For Dave and his family, gathering at our home and writing that obituary was gut-wrenching, surreal, and unfair—it was all the things death usually is. How do you choose what to say about this person that hasn't been said about everyone else who has been taken too soon? *Paul was loved by many.* True. *Paul was an avid outdoorsman.* True. *Paul was too young to die and damn it, maybe his best years were yet to come.*

Aren't most of our loved ones taken too soon? Even when a great-grandmother of 101 or something wild like that passes after a drawn-out battle with a terrible disease, don't we always remember the *one thing* we might have said to her or done for her if we only had one more day? When something amazing happens and our first thought is to share the news with the person who has departed, don't we feel like we've been robbed? Don't we want to smash things, even if we hardly have the energy to get out of bed and eat a bowl of rice our mom has made?

There's no sense in death, even if we know the facts of it.

Dave's parents lost a child; Dave and his siblings, Nina, Mark, and Joy lost their wild brother. All I could do was feed them while they gathered to grieve and prepared to mourn. All I could do for Dave afterwards was be there for him, and keep saying Paul's name. I had just lost my dad three years prior, so I had some understanding of what it is we need to hear, and not hear, after someone is taken from us. You say their name, even if there is a risk you'll open the flood gates, and even if those flood gates involve burning big embarrassing tears, or deep hard inner aches that threaten to double someone over.

A service for Paul was held in Hillsboro, Oregon. Mark officiated the service, as he would five years later for Dave. Dave read the obituary and friends and family got up and told stories about what Paul had meant to them. A few days later, we all travelled five hours to Prairie City, for Paul's burial service. We put together a slideshow set to some Jack Johnson songs and played it for everyone who gathered in the hall. Lots of folks who had grown up with Paul came and lots of tears and laughs were shared.

Dave and I had gotten through my father's death together, and we worked through Paul's death together too. Brad and Bryce, who had known Paul for just over a year, lost a playful uncle who had spoiled them, but because they were surrounded by lots of little cousins that week, they made it through okay. And Nina, who had started out as my friend but turned into family, to this day, we sometimes look at each other and without speaking, we think: *What the hell? Why the hell did all this death happen?*

⭐

"No one ever told me that grief felt so like fear."

~C.S. Lewis, Irish writer

When Brad and Bryce first came to live with us, their fear was palpable. We regularly had to assure them that the cupboards were full, the doors were locked, the dog would protect them. They would go to school with clean clothes every day, cool notebooks, and lunch money. They could bring friends over, they could run wild, they could snuggle with us.

On the *Holmes and Rahe Social Readjustment Rating Scale* (aka, the stress scale) for adults, Death of a Spouse is ranked the #1 Stressor. I would come to know such stress fully, and as an adult, would plod through it with every tool I could grab onto—even though the tools for widows my age felt scarce and flimsy. I was raised Catholic, but religious lit-erature and the notion that "Dave was an angel taken for a reason" would not pull me through, and I knew it.

On the *Holmes and Rahe SRRS* that has been modified for non-adults, after the #1 Stressor—Death of a Parent—common stressors include "not making an extracurricular activity" and "going to college." Brad and Bryce were of course no where near college-age when Dave died in 2011, and not that I don't understand what it feels like to be last person picked for a team, but our boys had experienced the following stressors—and probably then some— from birth: neglect, separation from a parent, removal from home, eco-nomic stress, drug and alcohol abuse by a parent, a parent's incarceration, and death of a parent (their biological father died in 2001).

Dave's death was brutal enough for me and the boys, but compounded with what I knew about foster children and PTSD—and triggers—with the PTSD itself looming, and then showing, I'm amazed we all made it. (Foster care "alumni" have a higher PTSD rate [it's 21%] than U.S. war veterans).

We did make it, thanks to family, friends, work col-leagues, and community, but I think the boys made it through—with some enormous bumps, to be sure—thanks to the six years we had as a family—as Dave, Melissa, Brad, and Bryce.

Other than working from home on Mount Emily taking its toll, I have to say, we lived a pretty stress-free existence. In the six months leading up to Dave's death, we were tak-ing family vacations, celebrating our favorite holidays, and making plans to get off that damn mountain in 2011 and move closer to town. We were going to have full-fledged neighbors. We would be just minutes from the kids' school. I would be less lonely.

To think in 2010, I had no idea what true loneliness was.

In Fall 2011, Dave was going to become the official high school football coach, and I was going to start leading the pep band—it was a gig I was really looking forward to. Dave had brought such pride to the football players and the band players, and there was nothing like bundling up on those chilly Eastern Oregon nights to cheer the team on as they scored touchdown after touchdown. I secretly loved watching the rival coaches seethe. The band itself was incredible too—Dave had taught so many of them how to play—so essentially, all I would have to do was put the strongest leader in charge, herd cats with musical instruments coming out of their mouths, and whip up enthusiasm.

In the summer of 2010, when Dave and I decided on a plan for 2011, non-pioneer woman me was thinking, "Okay, just one more winter to conquer."

One last summer, one last fall, and one last winter was what I'd be given.

In July of 2010, Dave, the boys, and I took an epic two-week road trip.

In Yellowstone, we waited for geysers to do what they'd been doing for thousands of years like clockwork. We took pictures of pools the color of turquoise and gold. We stayed on the lookout for marmots, moose, wolves, bison, and bear.

We did what all stupid tourists do—and one day, got scolded for it. Strolling down one of Yellowstone's boardwalks, Dave and I had let Bryce get a little too close to one of the bison he was taking photos of. You get tricked sometimes, because even though you know that beast weighs a couple thousand pounds, here he is, just moseying around, practically walking the boardwalk with you. "He's used to us," you think. "He's not bothered. He knows he's in charge. And by God, his face is so fluffy and cute."

"For the love of God," the ranger who was giving a guided tour shouted, "If you love your child, get him away from that buffalo."

We did. We heard later in the lodge that a week prior, someone had been mauled to death by a bear. Bryce's eyes widened hearing that!

From Yellowstone, we drove north toward Coeur d'Alene, Idaho. Coeur d'Alene translates into "heart of an awl," dubbed for the reputation its Native American tribe, the Coeur d'Alene People, had for being shrewd traders.

North of Coeur d'Alene, and south of Lake Pend Oreille, we took the boys to Silverwood Amusement Park, the largest amusement park in the Pacific Northwest. We swam in the pool, breathed in that gorgeous Northern Idaho summer air—which smells like pine needles and log cabins—and rode the rides.

One ride will always haunt me.

Dave, the boys and I got in, buckled our seat belts, and went up, up, up—straight up. You know the ride? The car you're in slowly climbs a 90° vertical ladder-like structure. Your tension mounts with each jilt skyward. They pause you for one second at the top, and as soon as you are about to take a deep breath, they drop you. You scream the kind of scream you can only let go of on certain rides—it's primal. Bryce might have yelled out a curse word—I'm pretty sure I did too.

But what Dave said to me after that ride was this: *Now I know what it will feel like when I die.*

He wasn't being funny at all, and remembering that shook me up for a long time, after his death.

But we had no fear that summer. We were on a family vacation and the great wide west was ours. Once we got back home, we spent our final August on Mount Emily and then Dave and the boys started another school year. Halloween 2010 came, and we went to the scariest haunted house any of us had ever been to—I have yet to find one so well put on. Union community members took over a historic building and filled it with skeletons, zombies, and buckets of blood. I swear, I peed my pants a little when a guy with a chainsaw came running after me.

"Grief turns out to be a place none of us know until we reach it. We anticipate (we know) that someone close to us could die, but we do not look beyond the few days or weeks that immediately follow such an imagined death. We misconstrue the nature of even those few days or weeks. We might expect if the death is sudden to feel shock. We do not expect the shock to be obliterative, dislocating to both body and mind. We might expect that we will be prostrate, inconsolable, crazy with loss. We do not expect to be literally crazy, cool customers who believe that their husband is about to return and need his shoes."

~Joan Didion, *The Year of Magical Thinking*

Ten days before Dave died, there was a huge snowstorm. Our power was knocked out for three days. We heated the house with a wood stove, so we were warm, but because I worked from home, I had to have Internet. I was determined not to give up any of my precious vacation days to Mount Emily and Mother Nature, who had decided to team up against me.

We borrowed a friend's generator, and I worked. But the generator was so loud and it filled the house with a gaseous odor and at a certain point, I told Dave, "Fuck this. I'm going to my mom's in Portland and I'm not coming back until the snow melts."

I stayed put, of course. I shoveled snow, and then more snow, and then more. I shoveled snow off the roof and I shoveled snow to get to the car. Then, I shoveled snow off the car. At one point, so tired of shoveling, I accidentally hit my head on a branch and started crying. I was shoveling and crying, my face raw and burning, and Dave said, "I'm sorry."

Dave died on a Friday.

That morning, through ice and snow, he drove Brad to the school for a field trip. Brad's class had won the eastern division in a LEGO Robotics competition, and they were heading to Portland for the finals. I don't know if they competed or completed their round. The weekend is a blur to me.

That evening, Dave, Bryce and I went to a local pizza joint in La Grande with some friends. On the way home, I texted Brad and he didn't answer. I was a little worried, because it was his first time away from us. I missed him. The first meal the four of us had ever eaten together had been pizza. Not that I thought anything different that night about eating pizza, but I missed our oldest kid. He was on the other side of the state, in the city I loved, and I was proud of him. But we didn't buy him a cell phone so he could ignore us, and that's what I texted him. Later, he texted to tell me they had all been at the movies. Phew. Brad was a good kid. He was safe. He still loved me even though I was a pain in his teenage ass!

Dave and I had been asked to chaperone that trip to Portland, but because Bryce had a basketball game Saturday and Dave was going to help out, we declined. Part of me, naturally, will always wonder, "What if..."

I wonder, what if all the "What if" lists in the world were collected: What would the top ten *What ifs* be? How many *What ifs* total would there be? Who would have the longest *What if* list? Would women have more *What ifs* than men? What would be voted the Most Heartbreaking *What if*? What sad soul would earn the Most Guilt-Charged *What if*?

What if Dave and I had gone that day to Portland? What if Dave and I had gotten off the mountain that summer instead of planning to the next? What if it hadn't snowed, or hadn't snowed so much? What if the day before, when Dave was complaining about "feeling congested," he had gone to the doctor? What if that night, I had been sleeping with him?

The night Dave died, after pizza and after contacting Brad in Portland, he told me he still wasn't feeling well. I gave him some Mucinex. Bryce and I got into our pajamas and pulled out the sofa bed. Dave kissed me on the cheek, saying he didn't want to get me sick, and Bryce and I started watching *The A-Team*, with Bradley Cooper.

Every other night of our life together, I had slept with Dave—whether one of us was sick or not. That night though, Bryce and I hunkered down and fell asleep on the sofa bed after the movie.

What if, right?

The next morning, I put more wood on the fire and let Bryce sleep in. I let the dog out and fed him, and by eight-o-clock or so, I thought, "Dave should be up."

I started gathering laundry from the boys' rooms, then made my way into ours, picking a few things off the floor. Then I saw Dave's leg. It was sticking out from under the covers; it was gray.

I went over to the bed and saw that his eyes and mouth were open. His entire body was gray and his fingers had started to curl towards his palms. I touched him. He was cold. He was stiff. I started to scream and shake.

I couldn't find my cell phone. I called out to Bryce, "Where's my phone?" He asked what was wrong. I told him to stay in the living room, to stay on the sofa bed.

I remembered we had a landline for my work—a miracle. I called 911. The dispatcher asked me to do CPR. I knew Dave was dead, but I did it anyway.

The dispatcher asked me who I could call to come to me immediately. I told her I didn't have my cell phone. I didn't know anybody's phone number by heart. I gave her the name of Dave's brother, Mark. She reached him.

In those first few minutes after hanging up with the dispatcher, my priorities were to keep Bryce from seeing Dave and… maybe… I don't know… maybe to breathe. I think I was still screaming. I think Bryce was screaming back at me, "What is it? What's going on?"

I went to Bryce, still in his little PJs, and I put my arms around him. I was shaking so hard he shook too. "I'm so sorry," I told him. "Your Dad has died."

Then, and this is a strange thing, I remembered a conversation Dave and I had had just a month prior. "If anything ever happens to me, Melissa," he'd said, "hide the weed."

Dave had been a private man and a respected and beloved school teacher, but yes, he smoked pot. The sheriff was on his way. People would be in the house. Looking back on it, I'll always think "What a strange thing to do," but after making sure to tell Bryce to stay put, I went into the garage and methodically bagged Dave's stash. And then, I bagged it again and stapled it all shut. "Okay, Dave," I thought. "I'm doing what you told me to do."

And throughout it all, in my head I was still screaming and pleading and crying out to everyone in heaven who had already gone—my dad, Paul, the boys' biological father, "Please, no, don't let this be happening. Don't take him now."

There was still so much we had to do.

Maybe I thought when I looked out the window and watched Dave's people start to arrive—his brother then his parents and his sisters—then my mom, brother with his wife, Erin, with their kids and Brad who they had picked up in Portland—maybe I thought I could have taken twenty-five more lonely-assed lethal ice and blinding snow winters. But no. No, I didn't think that. I was no pioneer woman and the boys needed their dad. Why did he go? That's what I thought when I was able to think again. I think.

"I wasn't prepared for the fact that grief is so unpre-
dictable. It wasn't just sadness, and it wasn't linear.
Somehow I'd thought that the first days would be
the worst and then it would get steadily better—like
getting over the flu. That's not how it was."

~Meghan O'Rourke, American writer

According to the U.S. Census, somewhere around 700,000
women lose their husbands each year. Surviving spouses
are at greater risk of dying—dying of a broken heart is
real. Surviving spouses isolate, lose their support base, and
sometimes fall into extreme poverty.
    For non-adults:

"One bereaved in five is likely to develop a psychiat-
ric disorder... the highest rates are found in boys."
(Journal of Child Psychology, October, 2000).
    "In a survey of 300 incarcerated teens, 96% in-
dicated that someone significant in their lives had
died." (Columbia University)
    "Between 5% and 7.5% of all children are active-
ly grieving." (US Census Bureau)

I'm filling the pages of this chapter with quotes and statistics
because, first of all, you normally don't go around record-
ing your happy life—all the days and moments before your
husband dies suddenly. We took a Yellowstone vacation, we
dressed up for Halloween, and we spent Thanksgiving at my
brother Mike's house, like we always did. We built snowmen
and shoveled snow and lit candles when the power went out.

We had a Christmas tree and ate Christmas cookies and celebrated New Year's Eve 2010. Maybe we made resolutions, maybe not.

I'm filling these pages with what others have said about grief, because when you lose someone, at some point, you want to devour all the grief words. You know you aren't the first one to experience this loss, but when it *feels like you are*, words from anyone who can describe the void in a way you can't, are consoling.

I include here all these other words because I heard everyone that loved me and loved Dave and loved the boys, in those first few days and weeks and months, choke on words—sometimes not knowing what to say. "I don't know what to say," or "Words can't express my sympathy," or, "I'm afraid I'll say the wrong thing."

It is so hard for the grieving to speak amongst themselves, and it is so hard for those outside the circle of grief to speak. I'm surprised the town of Union didn't turn mute for twenty-four hours. Maybe they did. I was on the mountain and the mountain was on me.

But silence is okay and saying the wrong thing is understandable. Having others keeping it real and simple, for me anyway, seemed key.

After Dave's death, a friend wrote me a note saying she would walk alongside me and the boys in our "grief journey," which, she said, was "sure to be very hard." I didn't understand what that meant at the time, or exactly how hard our journey would be, but it was a beautiful thing to read and it comforted me.

My childhood best friend's mom, Helen, reached out too. She had also experienced the death of her husband suddenly at age forty-four. I'd seen Helen about a year before Dave died, and had said to her: "I don't know how you did it. Jane and I were teenage girls; we were a handful!" I had told her that day that I thought she was amazing for having raised Jane and her two siblings after Don died.

Personal notes helped. Pre-printed cards with a simple handwritten sign off, "So sorry" or "If there is anything we can do..." helped. Someone sharing with me what someone already familiar with grief and mourning had written or said was okay too, *eventually.*

I've stuffed these pages with other people's words that *do* have meaning, and with statistics that have no meaning at all—until they swallow *you*—because it is hard to write about Dave's death, despite the years that have passed and the healing I have done and the new love I have now. It is hard to discuss death and grief in the United States. It is hard to discuss death and grief, period.

People came to us immediately that Saturday in January. Our house on Mount Emily filled within the hour after Dave died. When the paramedics arrived, I went into our bedroom with them. I watched them, hopelessly, check him for signs of life. "I wasn't in the bed with him last night," I told them. "What if...?"

What if he had shown signs of distress and what if I'd been able to get him into a seated position and what if my cell phone would have been right there where it always was on the bedside table and what if I could have called 911 last night and...

I don't know if they truly knew, but they told me, "There was nothing you could have done."

"But, CPR?"

"No. Nothing."

At some point, I'm not sure when, I called our friend, Damon, and told him we wouldn't make the ten o'clock basketball game. I told him what had happened. The game was cancelled and he came to the house immediately.

Bob and Shannon, our Union friends, and Dave's mother, stepfather, and brother Mark had already arrived. When, in the foggy chaos that was that morning, the paramedics went to wheel Dave's body out of the house in a body bag, Shannon and I took Bryce into Brad's room—there was no way any of us could bear witness.

Bryce, that morning, did not leave my side. We must have been moving and acting like a mama deer and her fawn in the headlights, but at some point I told him, "We have to call your brother, Brandon."

After I broke the news to Brandon, he asked me to put Bryce on the phone. Bryce was sitting in Dave's office chair. I don't know what Brandon said to his little brother, but that's when the biggest tears I had ever seen him cry came. An hour later, Bryce broke out in hives. For several weeks, he wouldn't shower unless I sat in the bathroom with him. I would sit and talk. I'd towel him off. He was eleven, but obviously—and for obvious reasons—he was regressing.

"Are you going to get married again?" he asked me once, when I was helping him get dressed.

It was a 2x4 to the head—his innocent question.

"I'm not thinking about that right now," I said.

Two weeks later, he asked me again.

"What's going on?" I said.

"I just want a dad."

I knew, of course, Bryce's desire for a solid male figure did not diminish his love for Dave. From the moment we'd adopted him, he was a child who knew what he wanted and was very good at asking for it. Still, it took all my resolve not to break down.

"I know, honey. And I'm so sorry."

It was all I could do or say at the time: *I'm so sorry.* This is what people were saying to me too: *I'm so sorry.*

Again, the order and timing of everything that happened the morning of Dave's death is a blur—who did I call first, second, third, tenth? But I do know that after I hung up with Damon, after telling him why our family would not make the basketball game that morning, it hit me: I had to reach Brad at that LEGO tournament in Portland before Damon gave the kids and their parents the news—and someone texted him a "So sorry" message.

I somehow got Greg on the phone, the teacher in charge of the field trip. Greg would write to me, years later when I asked him about that morning, the following:

I try not to think a lot about the day Dave died. Dave was someone I cared for and respected greatly. I also appreciated, so much, what he brought to the school, the community, and the kids. He was fantastic and we needed fantastic. I still miss him and think of him often.

As you can imagine, it was hard on Brad. He cried. Not uncontrollably or hysterically, but like he was deeply hurt, scared, and confused. I am sure it didn't help that I was crying as well. I remember having to find a spot in the massive school that was quiet, but that had cell phone coverage. A lot of the building did not have both. I managed to find a place with windows up on the second story, away from the hundreds of people that where there.

I remember when you got off the phone with Brad, and he was crying and I was crying, and I didn't know what to say or do. He was hurting and I wanted to make it stop, but knew that no one could.

I won't even pretend to know how Brad felt or what was going through his head. I remember asking him a couple of times if there was anything I could do, or if he needed anything. The answer was always a quiet "no." I remember at one point, I went and got him a bottle of water. Other than that, I just remember sitting by that window and waiting for his ride to show up to get him.

Once Brad got picked up, I went back to the rest of the kids. They were also all very sad. I have no doubt that day is a day my daughter Bayly will never forget.

⊶+⊷

"The only courage that matters is the kind that gets you from one minute to the next."

~Mignon McLaughlin, American Journalist

My mom, brother Mike, his wife Erin, and their kids picked Brad up that Saturday morning in Portland. Erin told me later that they scooped Brad into the backseat, and her kids engulfed him with warmth and love all the way home, across a white, silent, icy Oregon.

CHAPTER FOUR

Most of the grief literature tells you not to make any major life decisions after a loved one dies, but I made the major life decision to move us the hell off Mount Emily that first week. There was no way I'd be able to plow the driveway, get the boys to school in town on time, and then return to the house to spend my days alone. I couldn't touch that snow shovel I'd cried over just ten days prior ever again.

Our friends couldn't take care of us up on the mountain—and even though I am normally a person who has a very hard time admitting I need help and asking for it, I knew I'd need a ton of support following Dave's death.

Being a small town, Union didn't exactly have a wide array of rentals large enough for one woman, two boys, a dog, and all our toys, in the middle of winter, but I chose a place with enough square footage—sight unseen—and a week after Dave died, the town showed up at the mountain house, packed everything, and moved us to where they could all check in. A day or so prior, a whole crew of friends scrubbed the rental to its bones—figuring, they told me later, the "odd smell" would disappear. Rentals always carry a bit of an "aura" of the people who lived there before you, and I was in no state those first few days to care about "pleasantries." Friends unpacked for us. Friends kept the boys busy. My mom cooked for us and put a few Glade PlugIns around the house.

But then, you know—I could not breathe.

"Bob," I said, "Can you figure this stench out?"

Bob and Shannon were my touchstone after Dave died. The four of us had grown close—our kids hung out and we played Pinochle and bowled together. They helped arrange the funeral. Even with all my mom was doing, I would have been paralyzed without them.

Bob showed up for me immediately and tracked the scent, discovering the worst of all things: *dead cats*. There was a hole in the foundation of the rental that the town's feral cats could slip into, but could not escape.

I can look back on the dead cats now and say: Clearly, we weren't meant to live in that house, but at the time, when Bob told me what he'd found, I might have screamed bloody murder if I didn't think at the same time I would begin to vomit or sob uncontrollably. Within another few days, my friend Kris told me there was a house for sale across the street from her that wasn't selling. We made arrangements with the owner to show the place if need be, and moved in.

Brad, Bryce, and I were now safely tucked in to the town of Union, across the street from our friends Kris and Dan— within shouting distance even! This would have felt great under normal circumstances, but it was nothing short of a total lifesaver given the circumstances. The boys and I would live out the remainder of the school year in a nice clean home in the center of town. We could walk to everything; we could breathe.

We could also play, and cry, and talk with our friends. We were so fortunate to have made so many friends in that town, and a lot of that was thanks to Dave and the way he had worked with kids and recruited their parents.

Bob of the heroic and awful cat house duties had considered Dave one of his best friends. Dave had asked Bob to help with Bryce's baseball team: "You're a Dad," Dave said, "Let's co-coach our boys."

We were only in our thirties or early forties. Our kids played in Little League and attended LEGO conventions. Dave was supposed to see his boys go through sporting wins and losses, first loves and heartbreaks, college essays and acceptances, first jobs, and maybe one day, marriage and parenthood. We are all going along with all of those expectations, taking them 100% for granted—and in a way, we have to. If we thought even just once a week at what the ramifications would be if we lost our spouse or a child, how could we get on with our days? We couldn't. And then one day, we must.

We are fortunate beyond measure when that day does come, if we have community. Yes, people die of broken hearts, but what our community gave us after Dave died was a wide, strong, soft, welcoming cushion where all the shattered pieces could fall.

While Bob and Shannon came over for me, to ground me and pull me out to all the games and town events, Bob really stepped in as a male figure for Brad and Bryce. We miss each other.

That love the boys and I received in the last half year we stayed in Union buffered us, but of course, it also felt at times entirely impossible to function. I was grateful, in some ways, for the endless terrible paperwork: You call the student loan and credit card companies and you explain what happened. "Oh, we are so sorry," they say. (And then you have to make them feel better.) Paperwork gave me something to do; it allowed me to practice saying, "My husband has died."

Dave hadn't made a will either—we were young—so talk about paperwork! There was business to take care of in that regard and since I was always so good at "taking care of business," I honed in on it. I talked to the teachers' union and the PERS people; I got the truck registered in my name and paid off. Everyone needed a copy of the death certificate—I must have sent out a dozen.

My brother Mike and Dave's sister Nina would be Brad and Bryce's guardians, we had talked about that before, and after Dave's death, I solidified all of that legally, dotting every "i" and crossing every "t." I couldn't die on them now, that was for damn sure.

Post-death paperwork, for me, was something of a life raft. The forms with their blanks and bubbles, boxes and signatures required—consume you. The adoption paperwork had been similar, although of course, a lot more inspiring. Death paperwork prolonged my acknowledging the depth of my pain, I knew this. I knew I was in shock, and was numb. And at the same time, my heart was palpitating like crazy.

I'd been diagnosed with a benign irregular heartbeat in my thirties, but for years it had subsided. Two days after Dave died, I called my doctor, told her Dave had died, and said: "My heart is skipping beats," and she told me, "You need to get in here now!"

So, Monday after I went to the funeral home to make funeral arrangements, I went to my doctor.

"I can't have a heart attack now," I told her. "I can't do that to Brad and Bryce."

I can only imagine what I looked like. Not that anyone would have cared or judged, except a doctor. The first question she asked was: "Have you slept at all?" No, I hadn't, not for forty-eight hours.

Immediately, I was sent to the hospital for an EKG. In the meantime, my doctor told me she wanted me to take an anti-depressant that also induced sleep—temporarily. I was so numb, and didn't want to feel number. I didn't want to take pills; I never had. But of course, I knew I needed to sleep. I agreed to take half pills when necessary, and because my EKG showed some irregularities, I would wear a heart monitor for three days. When I felt my heart skipping beats, I was supposed to record the time and what I was doing, but I didn't. What was I doing, besides checking off boxes and wandering through minutes of the day like a zombie?

I turned in my heart monitor on Thursday, with zero patient notes (the doctor could have scolded me, but I don't remember if she did or didn't, and I doubt she did). On Friday morning, we held Dave's funeral, and on Friday afternoon my doctor called: "We saw you had an irregular heart event on Wednesday. What was going on between 6-8 PM?"

Wednesday evening was when I saw Dave's body at the funeral home—when I'd brought the boys there with me. My heart was pounding and skipping beats like crazy. Keep that in mind, if you aren't someone who'd normally be hooked up to a heart monitor.

A couple weeks later, as follow-up, my doctor ran a stress test and sent all my paperwork to a cardiologist for review. I was given the green light. "You're fine," they told me, "but we'll keep monitoring you for a few months."

Was my broken heart mendable? Definitely not. All these years later, I wouldn't call myself "cured." I'm still a jumpier person than I was prior to Dave's death, and my naturopath says I'm still in "fight or flight" mode. She works with me on combinations of supplements to mellow me out.

Grief is miraculous though, in its own dreadful way. With so many people visiting and filling our days, for a while I was able to tell myself that Dave was just on vacation. Our friends and our families were talking about him so much, it didn't seem like he was *gone* gone. I cannot stress how much this talk helped the boys and I. It might not be "recommended"—the delaying of reality—but after a sudden and shocking death, I think the collective spirit of buoyant goodwill works at an almost biological level to help the grieving survive.

"We won't let him die, no, we won't," is how it feels, even if everyone saying it and thinking it recognizes they are using the wrong verb tense.

But my mom did eventually have to leave us, and she did in February, right before Dave's birthday. (I still have a really hard time getting through winters—I could move to Hawaii and still feel the ache.)

How do you celebrate that first birthday after death? What does a dead loved one's "birthday" come to mean? Why don't you realize before someone dies, the intense value in taking one day a year to say, "I'm grateful you swam fastest and popped out into this wild world X-long years ago. Hoorah to your parents for making you! Hoorah for being my best friend!"

The reality nobody would ever see Dave again didn't hit me until my mom left—it didn't hit me until I set out three plates for dinner the first time, instead of four.

I wanted to acknowledge Dave's birthday February 17th, so we each wrote a little note, and I put them in helium balloons, and we let them go. I kept copies of the notes; I still have them.

I have a box of mementos, but again, so much of those first few weeks flew by in a memory-erasing blur. For the most part, that's just fine with me—although, at times I think it'd be nice if I could remember all the incredible things people did for us. Of course, I do remember that because there was no will, I had to charge Dave's funeral on my credit card. I do remember that my work colleagues, our friends and family gave thousands of dollars for Dave's scholarship fund and that people from all over gave us care packages of food and games. People drove across a brutally icy Oregon to attend his funeral.

I do remember saying to people at the reception: *I can't believe you're here.*

I have the program notes from Dave's funeral. Someone had offered to record it, and in my state of utter disbelief, denial, pain, anger, and brokenness—whatever that hell is that first week—I said, "No." The only reason I think now I maybe should have said, "Yes," is so I could remember the beautiful bits of it. You hear things said that you think you knew or felt, but to hear them from another person's mouth is truly priceless. You hear descriptions of the person who has died and think: "I never would have used that word about him, but wow, if it isn't exactly *right*!?"

Truth is, although I hardly remember any of the specifics of those hours, I do remember not wanting to walk into that gym, and almost not being able to walk. My legs were shaking and I wanted to come out of my skin. I wanted to flee so bad that I think the only thing that kept me from doing so was the grip I held on the boys' legs. Brad was crying, I remember this, because I did not see him cry at any other time.

Dave's brother, Mark, is a pastor and he presided over the funeral. My brother Mike wrote a eulogy and read it, while Dave's family, my mother and I, the boys and their brother Brandon, sat there shaking. My sister-in-law Erin read the obituary, and she broke down. Dave's best friend, Mike, the only guy Dave ever got in a fight for, spoke too. The school principal and a teacher spoke—maybe two or three teachers spoke, I can't remember. I imagine they said things like we had said at Dave's brother's funeral and at my father's funeral: *He was a great man. He loved his family. He had so much left to give or do. We'll miss his laugh.*

━━┽┼━━

Within those first few hours after Dave's death, the idea of having a glass of wine or smoking a cigarette sounding utterly disgusting. Not that I was a heavy smoker or a wino or anything, but everything simply lost its appeal—everything tasted terrible. It's true: The boys and I lived for the plain white rice my mom made us. My mouth was so dry the only thing I ate for days was applesauce.

And while I monitored my skipping heart, we watched the boys. What on earth can you expect your children to do when your spouse dies? How can you be strong and entirely exposed—vulnerable, afraid, desperate—at the same time?

Pre-funeral, when we were packing, the house was full of commotion. Above the sound of packing tape being ripped across boxes and the folding of newspaper around plates and glasses, my mother told me later that she had heard a ruckus in Brad's room. Brad hadn't raged the way he had that first month Dave and I adopted him ever again, but anger would always be his go-to emotion—he is still a work-in-progress in that regard, the way I am a work-in-progress in terms of letting go.

But there he was, my mother said, in the days between Dave's death and the ceremony in which we would honor his life, standing in his room, throwing stuff all over the place. My mom went in—she didn't want to bother me with it—and she sat with him and let him be sad and destructive.

That same week, Bryce got mad at me. For what, I'm not sure—maybe I had been cross with him, I don't remember, but in the midst of packing, I found that he had torn up a photograph of he and I at Disneyland.

"What's going on?" I asked him. "Why'd you do this?"

Bryce was ten (he turned eleven, eleven days after Dave died), and I could see instantly he felt sad about what he'd done. Luckily, I always got two sets of photos, and I told him I'd replace the one he'd torn. I let him know if he was mad at me, it was okay. I told him I was mad at me too. I told him I was sorry if I'd hurt his feelings or if I was stressed and cranky over the past few days—and that if I had, it was only because everyone was having such a hard time. We were all having such a hard time together. Brad and Bryce knew hard times—the difference now was, I like to think, they had a large loving clan to turn to.

Our clans rallied, but I also intuited that once the initial shock wore off and I began to fully grieve, I might need extra support doing the "mom thing." I had struggled at times to feel like a fabulous mother *before* Dave died. As I've said, he was my rock and always my "go to" confidence builder. Those days when I doubted if I was keeping up with the Mrs. Jones' or not, Dave always reassured me. My family and friends did too, but without Dave, how the hell was I going to parent?

How do you parent two young children through yet another incidence of shock and grief?

When we got to Portland months later, I would take the boys to the nationally renowned *Dougy Center*, where they could hang out with kids their age and grieve—where they could get solid, professional, steady counsel. I had Googled the center while we were still in Union, and consumed as much information as my brain and heart could handle. I had to move through this, and so did our boys.

The boys and I did take advantage of some of the *Dougy Center's* offerings, but therapy was not Brad nor Bryce's cup of tea, and I wasn't going to force it. Dave and I never had. So, the boys played their grieving ping pong games and we split into our parent and kid groups and talked things out, but eventually I kept going back to the resources I found most useful—books on grieving that I downloaded on my Kindle.

After Dave's death, we received so many incredible care packages. People sent DVDs and vats of delicious chocolate covered popcorn, they sent cards and photos and books. Faith-based grieving literature didn't work for me at all though: I can't jibe with those who say, "An angel has been taken," or "God wanted him on his team." That's not me, and it wasn't Dave either. It's not to deny comfort to anyone who finds such sentiments comforting, but it's the Joan Didion grieving reality—and writing—I'm much more in tune with.

I'm Grieving as Fast As I Can was sent to me, and I'm grateful. Every page was filled with no-nonsense advice that allowed me to say, "Oh, so I'm *not* going crazy? Phew!"

You are not going crazy. You are not. Find the people whose words and wisdom and presence assure you of this, because at times you will feel like you will never be sane again—not teenage girl with your best girlfriends slumber party nutso, not falling in love for the first or second time off-the-rails or walking down the aisle wild-eyed, not discovering you are pregnant or that you-can-never-get pregnant-stunned. The death and grieving crazy train arrives and departs from an entirely different station and it will run you over at times and in places you can never foresee or control or run from. But trust me, *you are not crazy.*

Trust yourself that your life can and will go on—the movie screen will not stay dark forever.

Read books like *Widows Wear Stilettos*—which is practical and funny. Yes, laugh whenever you can because laughing while grieving does not mean you are crazy. You want to go crazy? Okay, *go crazy*, thrash about and throw some (soft and unbreakable) items around your basement. Talk to your deceased loved one, talk to God, or talk to your dog (my dog, Buxton, saved my hide). Cry until your eyes tire of crying, but you are not crazy. Death fucking sucks!

I do believe in a higher power, that is, I started to believe in one after Dave died, but for the most part, I just wanted to feel that there were other people who had been through what I was going through. I wanted to know I would get past the deep pain and numbness. I wanted to learn how to dig into the pain so that I would come out whole on the other side. If anything from the "faith-based" material did comfort me, it was the notion that Dave and I would see each other again. I don't necessarily mean I believe he'll come to me like Patrick Swayze did with Demi Moore in *Ghost*, but he does come to me—his energy is here always.

The boys had come to us without much religious schooling, and that wasn't going to change. Again, we weren't anti-church, we just found a lot more awe and healing, I guess you could say, in nature and in us. We played in the great outdoors together as a family—what is more sacred than that? The boys learned so much about right and wrong, practice and fair play—and miracles—through the sports Dave coached them in.

The Thursday after Dave died, Bryce insisted on playing in a basketball game.

When I say that everyone came to that game—I do mean everyone! Bryce played one of his best games ever. He made one shot, and it was magical. It might sound straight out of an after school special, but he actually said, "I did that one for Dad."

I didn't look around, but I guarantee there wasn't a dry eye in the gymnasium after that.

The boys never missed a beat in terms of showing up for their teams. They didn't want to stick around at home and be sad. I'm grateful for that. Their remaining active gave me time to figure out how to keep my own forward momentum; it gave me time to read up on how to help them when and if despair hit the fan. I tried to make things as normal as possible. They took one week off of school after Dave died, but that was it. They wanted to go to school the following Monday, so I walked them there.

The boys needed that routine, but when I announced that we were moving to Portland, they took that in stride as well. We'd had multiple conversations about all the friends and family we had back there, so moving was not a shocker to them. They were both sad to leave their teams and friends behind in Union, but in truth, though Brad never told me explicitly how he felt, he had always seemed somewhat more like me in that we both craved the city life. Bryce could go with any flow—the kid could probably live in a yurt in Mongolia, or on a space colony on the moon.

Yes, I needed Portland. Like Brad, I'd made great friends in Union, but my closest people were on the other side of Oregon. I knew too, that after taking some time off work (I took a three-day bereavement and a five-week short term disability leave—ridiculous—because I wasn't actually even able to grieve at that point)—eventually I needed to get back to working in a real office again, with real colleagues, desks, windows, white boards, and swivel chairs.

I'd have work again, workmates, and the familiar sidewalks of the Rose City. The boys would adjust to new schools, new friends, and new teammates. They'd have their aunts, uncles, cousins, and my mom. The boys and I would have each other—and Buxton.

I've never actually thought about how differently Dave's death would have affected me if he and I had never adopted. I do know though, that because of the boys, I could never just pull the covers over my head. I needed to be on it. My head was fuzzy and my heart was not behaving, so, more than ever, I had to stay clear. I didn't touch cigarettes, wine, or beer for months. It didn't sound good. I would go through days and weeks where I felt nothing and would eat very little, but at least that nothing was a clear nothing.

<hr>

Dave was gone. I wasn't going to see him again. In a way, I was counting down the weeks to Portland, but I was also trying to live each day as it came to me. I went walking a lot, taking advantage of finally living in town. Yes, Dave and I were supposed to be walking these sidewalks together—it's what we had been visualizing.

Past lives, the afterlife, Heaven or no Heaven, angels, and saints, and demons—who knows. Life and death can be equally mysterious. I would talk to Dave after he died and would ask him questions, because after so many years together, you don't just stop the dialogue. Dave would answer me most of the time, via music, usually a lyric. *Brick House*, a song that his band played, hits me and all of our friends like, well, a ton of bricks—but of course, we always dance to it. That's what—here comes the comforting cliché—that's what Dave would have wanted us to do.

I would talk to Dave in my mind, mostly, asking him to give me a sign, point me in the right direction, enter the boys' hearts and help them, or put the right person, website or book in my path. He was my higher power in a weird way; he was who and what I believed in. I've said he was no saint, he was not a chosen angel of any God I'm familiar with, but he represented love, loyalty, and joy. He did what was best for his family and community. He was an Oregonian through and through too—he loved his tunes, his teaching, his beer, and his outdoors.

One early spring morning—it was the morning I had decided 100% the boys and I would move back to Portland—I was on a walk. The sun was shining, and all of a sudden, I experienced the overwhelming scent of cloves. *"What?!"* I thought. Dave used to smoke cloves.

I stopped and whirled around. It was 6:30 in the morning. Even heavy smokers don't usually walk around at that hour smoking cloves. I didn't know anyone in Union who smoked cloves, and besides, nobody was around—not a living soul, anyway. I looked for a plant or flower and even bent over to sniff a few. Nothing. So this quick short burst of clove cigarettes—you tell me. I started crying on the spot. I said out loud, "Oh my God, thank you, you're still here."

It hadn't been the first time I'd hoped Dave would give me "a sign" when faced with a tough decision, but it was the first time he so clearly came to me to say, "Yes, go with your gut."

I am fairly skeptical: If a thing is not in front of me, I'm not sure it exists. I don't doubt Dave understood I still needed him, so he showed up. I still do need him; I still do ask his guidance; and he still guides.

⭐

People say careless things after someone dies. They don't mean to, but it is so true that most of us don't know how to approach death, mourning, and grief. Maybe it's because of fear—fear of not knowing what lies beyond that door, and fear of being left behind.

The grieving too, feel they shouldn't be out "spreading their pain or their doom or their suffering." We feel like we don't want to make others feel uncomfortable. How odd is it that it's the widows and widowers telling the credit card guys, "Hey, it's okay. We'll be fine."

How many calls of the "my spouse has passed away" type, do they take daily?

The grieving know that people are walking on eggshells around them, but that they must walk on eggshells too—we don't want to make others turn mute. Most of the time, yes, we also are acutely aware of everyone else's sadness, and because of this awareness—which is as circular and as powerful as a cyclone—we all try to spare anyone from feeling even sadder. It is so damn hard for everyone, and at times, we all feel like just saying FUCK IT—and that's *before* the "anger" phase of grieving even sets in.

But there are those days and weeks where you can just let it all hang out, where honestly, you have no choice in the matter, where whoever you run into might just be struck with this plain fact: Here I am, puffy eyed and uncontrollably weeping with snot running out of my nose, my face twist-ed into something even Picasso couldn't have dreamt up, and sounds exploding from my chest like an elephant has stepped on it.

There are moments in the abyss, under the elephant's foot, where you stop caring what others think of how you are processing death. You feel mad and crazy, but you do not care. You keep it together by a thread, and only for your children, and if you don't have children, maybe for your parents, or if you don't have any of that—maybe for your colleagues.

After Dave died, one thing I really stopped caring about was food. I dropped a ton of weight. It was never a danger, not any more than my heart palpitations and lack of sleep were, but one day, my wedding ring slipped off. Two and a half months after Dave died, there it was on the floor—a big golden zero, a shining empty hole, a piece of precious metal that symbolized eternity. Eternity? I was pissed. I picked my ring up, put it in a drawer, and did not wear it again.

I read later that this is a very personal thing—deciding when to remove your wedding ring for good. When mine fell off of its own accord, it isn't as if I took it as a sign ex-actly, but it hurt—*it meant something!* It was its own shock.

"I don't *feel* married anymore," I thought. "I don't want to resize my ring. What's the point?"

And yes, I would sometimes put my ring back on to see what it felt like, but what it felt like was this: I didn't have a partner that was alive anymore.

I felt self-conscious at first: I could see and feel people noticing it. It's funny how naked a finger can feel. But it was the decision to keep that ring in a drawer that I can now see marked the start of me trusting my gut. I would have to make a handful of painful decisions after Dave died, and getting used to my bare left ring finger was one of the first of them.

Was it too soon? Not for me it wasn't. At a certain point—at several points, actually—the grieving have to say, "Others can think what they will, but nobody is walking in my shoes, nobody is feeling what I'm feeling, and the only thing that matters right now is that I am trying to do what is best."

This determination kicks in for some of us sooner than others, but once it does kick in, own it. This is not to say it feels wonderful 100% of the time after you declare, "I'll do it my way."

No, you will question *your way* of grieving and moving on from grief on a regular basis. You'll have your first decent day, and you'll feel guilty and wretched about it. What if you laugh too loud at a ball game only five weeks after your husband has died? What if you yell at your kid for something meaningless? All of the usual parental guilt and slight teenage-level self-consciousness that we all feel even in adulthood—while grieving? Yeah, multiply all that by a thousand.

There may be five or six or seven stages of grief, but there are a billion ways to move through it. We are all going to lose loved ones and we're all going to be the loved one that is lost, and none of us has a clue how one particular death out of the several that will crush us, will impact and change us. You cannot really walk in the griever's shoes, but you can offer them a place to rest their sore feet along the way to healing.

CHAPTER FIVE

Change in residence is fairly low down there on the *Holmes and Rahe Stressor Scale*: It packs a whopping twenty points, compared to one hundred points for death of a spouse. But while leaving Eastern Oregon felt bitter-sweet in many ways, it was also a huge release.

I had made the final decision to move back to Portland just a couple of months after Dave died, and my decision was sealed on that early morning walk when I was overcome by the scent of clove cigarettes. No matter what your religious bent—no matter if you have not one religious bone in your body—the universe tosses you signs. Dave was with me, and he knew that while the boys and I would have been happy enough staying in Union, Portland was where I would thrive most. I am a city girl after all, and Mount Emily taught me how ridiculous it was to keep trying to prove I was made of "heartier stuff."

Ice and snow, power outages and isolation—really? Walk into your bedroom to find your spouse dead and you learn quickly enough exactly what kind of stuff you are made of.

One of the things I have always been made of, for better or for worse, is the need to control my little corner of the universe. Before Dave died, this need was relatively mild, I mean, in general I don't do well with wishy-washy on-the-fence no-boundaries situations—which is one of the reasons working from home had been such a challenge for me—I need structure.

Controlling where I would live, work, and continue to seek support in terms of working through Dave's death, felt good to me; but after his death, I definitely went through stages of needing to control *more*. More what? Just *more*. Logically, I knew death—sudden death—could happen at any time to anyone. Logically, I also knew that checking in on the boys every night to see if they were breathing in their sleep would not keep them immortal.

Some of my desire to control more was just plain senseless and ironic, because it was Dave's death that made it glaringly clear none of us can ever truly control a single thing. Some of my desire to control more was beneficial: I needed to do anything and everything that made me feel good and I took control to make that happen.

Once I announced we would be moving at the end of that school year, everyone completely understood. Fortunately, or unfortunately, because of their lives in and out of foster care, the boys hardly even batted an eye! Brad, like I've said, seemed a bit relieved, because like me, he didn't feel like he fully fit in with small town life. So, Portland it was. I'd be sad in the City of Roses—in fact, I'd experience the deepest elements of my grief there as the shock and numbness would begin to wear off. I would be tackling deep-rooted issues as I explored the impact of Dave's death on the very structure of my reality and cells of my being; I would be struggling, no doubt, but at least I would be in my element.

In the months preceding our move, the boys and I purged a ton! There are all sorts of popular books out now on the value of holding on only to the things that bring you joy, but what mementos do you keep after death? Clearly, we kept the letters the boys sent up by balloon for Dave's first non-birthday birthday. We kept photo albums and sports gear and certain shirts and "trinkets" of Dave's. But when you are sifting and axing the contents of a 3000-square foot house to prepare for a comfortable life in a house one-third that size, bammo! You have no mercy.

The "experts" tell you to take time going through your loved one's thing, but once again, I broke the rules. A few articles of clothing, a few items from our earliest days together and later trips we took as a family—of course, I kept those. But furniture, books, sweatshirts, old fishing poles and tennis rackets—you give it all away.

Clear way for your new life, even if you don't want to see that eventually you will have to make one.

You don't have to go through some Burning Man level ritual in order to clean house and begin to move forward, but you can, I think, let go of things in a magical, meaningful way. What would Dave do with the two buckets of rocks he'd collected—have us cart them all the way across the state? *No.* I had the boys pick a few rocks they wanted to keep, and I kept one too—it is black, shaped like the state of Oregon, and sitting on Dave's memorial shelf in our house. It is cool to the touch and smooth—on really bad days, I can pick it up and hold it in my hand. Our objects can hold us.

But the rest of those rocks, the boys and I hauled up Mount Emily. We sat on the deck of our still-empty house overlooking all our trees, and chucked one after the other. We shouted when we hit a tree square, and we shouted when we missed a tree completely! We hooted and hollered. There was anger and love in the release. There was liberation in putting all those rocks Dave had touched, back where he had found them.

The rock throwing party was the first and last time I went up the Mount Emily with the boys. I don't know that they would have wanted to spend more time there. And for all the time I had spent wanting to move out of that house and never look back, I did go up several times alone, during my five-week "stress leave."

I would drive up the mountain and go through the house to see if I had left anything—although, probably after the third time there, I knew I'd cleared out every possible nook and cranny. The thing was: I felt Dave was still there. Maybe it's a crazy thing to worry that your dead spouse is somehow "lost" and wondering where everyone went, but if I could feel his presence, couldn't he feel the lack of mine and the boys'? I was talking to him in our little house in Union, and I talked to him too, in the Mount Emily house. What did I say? I don't know.

I do know that our house that had once been so full of our lives, had become as quiet and as still as the woods surrounding it. In my spring solo visits, whatever words I did say out loud carried differently than they had in the winter, and in all the previous seasons—when our hallways and walls held family portraits and our kitchen cabinets were stuffed full of snacks for the boys. The empty house began to smell different too—the air inside unfamiliar, no longer ours. It's a little weird, if you give too much thought to the human breath. Dave had lived and breathed as he stepped across this floorboard that creaked just so when you put your weight on it. He had sipped a beer here, and there too.

And all that firewood, chopped and stacked. How many calories had he and the boys burned on those days? Someone dies and you think of the way they snored and sweated, sang and danced. A bird flies from a branch and your eye follows. Dave? Those trees in the sunshine filled my head with pine. We had spent so many good summers camping as a family. Some mornings in Oregon, you swear you can smell the hearts of trees.

On my last visit up Mount Emily, solo, before moving to Portland, I did not go inside the house. I had looked at our empty bedroom enough—had remembered funny dinner conversations between the four of us. That last visit, I brought up a few of Dave's favorite beers and cracked one open. I hadn't had a beer since he died.

I brought my iPod too, thumbing the wheel to Pink Martini's *Over the Valley*. The song will always remind me of being in that house, with Dave and without him. I listened to Diana Krall's remake of *I've Grown Accustomed to His Face*. I sipped my IPA. Yes, I listened to every sad song my broken heart could handle, and when I got up to leave, I do remember what I said: I said, "Dave, if you are here, don't stay up here alone. Come with us."

There was, in fact, freaky evidence that Dave was still in that house—it wasn't just me who experienced it either. Our friend, Darren, who had the granite bench made that now sits at the *Dave Opperman Memorial Sports Complex,* came out in May 2011 from Portland with a few of our friends to deliver the bench. The guys all wanted to stay up at the empty Mount Emily house overnight to play music and hang out, so I let them in, set them up, and said, "Just don't burn the house down."

Dave had fought fires back in the day. I was joking with his friends, of course, but fire danger in Eastern Oregon come springtime is no laughing matter.

The next day, Darren and Donnie (Donnie had been on the island with us when Dave proposed) told me that after they'd hung out in the garage the previous night—where we all used to listen to music and party when we had guests—they had closed the garage windows. The next day, they found them all open four to five inches.

The garage windows at the Mount Emily house were heavy and clunky—there's no way once they were closed they could "randomly" defy gravity. I had found them open too, in past visits, and at first had worried we had a squatter or some kids coming around to party. But in all my times up there, I had never found a trace of foul play or actual "human" visitors. Nothing else was ever disturbed.

I'm not sure I ever told my mom about Dave's garage "visits," but either way, Mom, who is very Catholic, believed his spirit was with us. My mom was, in fact, the first person to direct me to my first psychic. About a year after Dave's death, I went and saw a woman who my mother's friend had seen after her son died. This friend told my mom the psychic knew things only a truly gifted person could know—they believed their son was in the room with them. So, of course, I wanted to see if Dave would appear, and I wanted to hear what he might say.

Death opens people up to alternative ideologies. Had I told my mom about my Mount Emily chats with Dave's spirit, or had I told her about his friends feeling like he had messed around with the garage windows that night, would she have instantly believed me? Would all her Catholic rules and lessons about the afterlife have flown out the window? Would she have worried about my state of mind—looked for other signs I wasn't moving along the path of grieving "appropriately?"

How many of us talk to the dead? When does talking to the dead just become talking to ourselves? How do any of us ever separate ourselves from those who have died? And who says we should? I say we keep the conversation going—because *what if?* Right? What if they can see things we can't? Or what if we can't see that *we see* things we can't, and in talking things through with our dead loved ones, we come to some core truth? Truth is good. Truth should guide us. In this crazy living world, I'm willing to take whatever form of magical beyond-the-knowing help I can get. And this is coming from someone who has learned to admit to having "control issues."

There is mystery—here and now and wherever we end up after death. Nothing can convince me otherwise. Maybe we can meet on another plane—astral or parallel or whatever you want to call it—one of us alive here on Earth and nowhere else, one of us dead here on Earth but alive elsewhere.

I certainly tried summoning Dave to me. About a year-and-a-half after his death, when I started to drink a little too much—and yes, I'll get to that eventually—I would sometimes smoke some of his stash of weed I hadn't thrown away. I ritualized it, using a little wooden pipe he kept in a fleece bag we'd bought together on a trip to Joseph, Oregon. *Dave's lips used to touch this pipe,* I would think, inhaling, exhaling, and waiting.

Even Mom had her own "odd" experience after Dave died. She was spending the night and at some point in the wee hours, she woke up because a light had turned on upstairs. Good old Buxton was snoring away at the foot of the King sized bed we were sharing—the bed Dave and I had shared for so many years—so Mom got up, walked downstairs to check on the boys, and found them fast asleep.

The next morning, she asked them if they'd been up at all during the night, and they answered, "No."

When we were alone a little later, Mom told me what had happened. We looked at each other quizzically for a split second, and then it dawned on me: "Oh, you were sleeping in Dave's spot! I bet he was wishing you a Happy Mother's Day."

She didn't miss a beat. She nodded.

I wished she had woken me up.

＝≺⊢⊣≻＝

Dave left Eastern Oregon with us, I'm convinced. I felt him regularly, and so did some of our closest friends. We still believe Dave guides us. He was a natural teacher and coach while he inhabited this planet, and spirit does not simply perish.

Does this mean I felt him constantly lurking over my shoulder and guiding my every move in Portland? Does it mean that two years after his death when I began to have the first glimmers of my life continuing on, perhaps with another man, I felt Dave hovering around and waiting to throw a fork across space like a poltergeist if and when another man tried to kiss me? Of course not.

But of course, I felt I needed some guidance to work through all the stages of grief and the colliding cycles of it. I did rely on a grief counselor - a seasoned professional - to tell me: "One day you won't feel guilty about believing you will live a very great life."

In addition to being that teacher, that coach, that husband and father, Dave had always been my best friend. He was a benevolent and loving person, so of course, he would want me to be happy again. But for a very long time, happy did not feel possible.

One of the first places I took the boys after settling back in Portland was the Dougy Center. The place is a rock for so many children and teenagers in need of grief counseling, and I'm grateful for our time there—even if, in reality, it seemed sports and family helped Brad and Bryce cope almost just as well. These kids had been through hell and back more than once, and except for a few glimpses into what would eventually become a serious behavioral matter with Brad, they seemed to be taking Dave's death with a fairly "typical" dose of sadness and grief.

I was worried about them, of course, but I was a lot more worried about myself. I had to stay strong, but I was beginning to feel like I was unravelling. I was developing obsessive worries about the boys at night—were they breathing?

How many times should I get up and check? Fears that I hadn't experienced prior to Dave's death—not even with my father's death—started to invade my existence. Logically I knew these fears served no one and could save no one, but I couldn't quell them. I would get out of bed after battling myself, and enter the boys' bedrooms to watch the moving of their chests up and down, up and down—okay, yes, they were still alive and dreaming.

The insomnia that came with those fears wasn't my only problem, and I knew it. It was Dougy Center staff that provided me with a list of three potential therapists. The first woman I called was Normina. She said: "I have an opening this week, come on in."

In July 2011, after a very brief conversation with Normina, I knew I liked her. She gave me a great rate (I had insurance, but she wasn't on my "in-network" list), and so we began. Normina was seventy-five years old when I first started working with her and at 4'10" she was tiny! But she had a nose piercing and bi-level haircut and a brilliant badass attitude, and I immediately felt comfortable with her. In our first session, after giving her the "nickel tour" of the past seven months, I said: "Okay. So, how does this work? Give me the steps."

She smiled. Clearly I had no idea about grieving the loss of a spouse, but I was nothing if not persistent.

"How about you give me some A-to-Z steps to get me through these five or seven stages of grief? Here I am now in Portland. I'm home. This is where I can go deep, start feeling better, and get over Dave's death. I'm ready! Please help."

Normina smiled again. She told me she was glad that Portland was my home and that the boys and I were surrounded by family and friends. She was glad to have me in her office. She said she was sure I understood grief as a process and sure I had cycled through some—if not all—of the stages of grief on my own in the past six months.

But, she added, "Here you are now. And here I am too, to tell you that grief is a process that takes work and I can't give you answers to the questions you just asked. I can only tell you that you will feel better and you will feel different and eventually, you will most likely be a better person than you thought you'd ever be."

"Okay," I said. "But out of all your years working with grieving widows, of my age and in the typical age bracket, how long does it take to get over grief? A few months? A few years? How long?"

"Melissa," she said, "that's not how grief works."

Normina and I arranged to meet weekly.

As wonderful as Normina was and as much as I trusted that it was, in part, Dave who was responsible for leading me to her (*"Lead me and the boys to the right people, Dave"*), it still took four months for me to completely trust this woman and to trust myself. Yes, in Union I had done a lot of reading and researching. I had Googled all the information one can Google on the stages of grief. I had taken online tests and surveys and monitored my own moods. I had kept busy. I had been learning. I had kept the boys going—mentally, emotionally, and physically.

Then four months into my work with Normina, I realized I had been going through the night of Dave's death on a minute-by-minute basis. For six months in Union, I had been in denial. I had been walking the line between functioning and getting shit done, and "a thousand heart-shattering *What Ifs.*"

When I was finally able to tell Normina that I could not stop my thoughts: "What if I had been in the bed with Dave that night?" Or better, "What if we had driven to the hospital that night after pizza?" Or hey, "What if we had been chaperoning that trip in Portland and had therefore gone to bed earlier or later?" or "What if...? " it was a huge relief. I knew from all my reading about widowhood that *what ifs* were normal, but when Normina said, "You are normal, Melissa," I practically collapsed with relief.

Normina helped validate so much of what I had been reading and ingesting all alone in Union. All of my *what ifs* were clearly elements I had no control over; in fact, this is the plain bare truth for all of our *what ifs*—yesterday's, today's and tomorrow's! Of course, realizing this, admitting this, coming to terms with this, practicing this, and living in this reality—we are all going to die and there is no *what if* about it—is not easy. Therapy helps.

My wishing I could have kept Dave alive was only the tip of the Melissa Controlling Iceberg. As I worked through my guilt and grief, I discovered I was wound pretty damn tight, and in many ways, I always had been. Toward the end of 2011, three seasons after Dave's death, I finally started letting go. When I tell you that it took me nine or ten months to allow myself to cry in front of people, I'm telling you that this was a major turning point in my forty-some years on earth. For the first time in my adult life, I learned it was totally acceptable and healthy *not* to try to hide my emotions from others. It was okay to appear *not* totally capable.

Wow! I could *own* my own emotions!

Of course, it was no surprise to anyone that *I was sad*, but it was amazing I could say it. This was new to me, and it was freeing as hell. Within a year after Dave's death, I began to stop worrying about what anybody else thought or wanted of me and for me. I tapped into my own gut, and what's more: I began to trust it.

In my two years in grief therapy, I learned that prior to Dave's death, I hadn't had to do much work around trusting myself, because I'd had Dave! I had a solid best friend and husband. Yes, we had our ups and downs like any normal couple, but the good times far outweighed the bad. I never questioned his loyalty or capabilities. I never questioned his love for me and the boys. I never doubted his work ethic or his creative talents. We laughed hard and had a social network that reflected the good life we had built together.

So the grief therapy I was in, morphed in and out of personal development therapy as well. Underneath all the strong solid framework of Dave and Melissa, and then of Dave, Melissa, Brad, and Bryce, I found cracks. And then I did not turn away from them.

Again, I'd had such a healthy upbringing, with a supportive mom and dad—so it had never seemed necessary to ask, "What is wrong with the Melissa picture?" If it ain't broke, why fix it, right?

But we are all a complicated mix of whole and broken bits. We can be fully loved and nurtured, but the world and our years muddling through it tear at us in ways we are often blind to. I discovered as I worked through missing Dave, that I carried feelings of guilt over not having spoken up for myself often enough—*with Dave!* I had never actually wanted to live in that Mount Emily house—not at all. But I did it to please my husband. I gave up my power. I had been giving up my power a lot throughout my life.

If I started to trust my own gut and live my life more in accordance with the way I wanted to live it, what the hell? What would it mean to be more fully accountable for my choices? What if I screwed up? It would all reflect on me! Who was I becoming? Was it normal and okay to be changing so much after Dave's death? And worst of all, what if I was becoming someone that Dave wouldn't like or want to be with?

Who would Dave and I be together? Would we work together now? I felt weird saying it, but Dave had had the power. We had been in a partnership, but some people are stronger than others. Now that I was beginning to know and like a lot more about myself than ever before, well... what would my life partner have thought? Would he recognize me? These thoughts made me sad, but they were also empowering.

I told Normina all of it, and again, she listened. Of course, she also spoke—about my control issues regarding the boys' breathing, or about Dave liking or not liking me today were he to walk through the door. She told me that what was happening was happening right now and I could not always make sense out of it. *You can only live this moment, and then the next and the next.* There is nothing you can do between moments to change a thing. There is nothing you can do about this past. You could not say ten years ago what you are saying today, and that's okay. Let this liberate you.

Eventually, focusing on the here and now did liberate me, and it still does. I still have to work on it. I even still sometimes wonder: "Yes, but would Dave like me today?"

And then I remember: I will never, ever know. Knowing is impossible. I can only let go of the guilt.

I remember: Dave was my partner for who I was then and Sean is my partner for who I am now.

━━◁┼ ┼▷━━

Guilt isn't easy to live with, or to release. We could write stacks of books on the topic, many do, but for *this* chapter in *this* book, I'll say this: I think every person who has lost a loved one can relate to having no clue on how to break past what you wish you had said or done (or not said or done).

But moving forward and doing the work, you do begin to understand the twisted nature of guilt and you do learn how to break its seemingly unrelenting grasp on your soul. You see that nine times out of ten, guilt serves no valuable purpose (and for those people who are serial murderers and chronic criminals or abusers, well, guilt doesn't even enter their minds, so why bother comparing apples to oranges?).

Freeing myself from guilt was hard work—it took weekly therapy sessions and long talks with a few other widow friends to finally be able to even begin to say: "Hey, Dave's not here right now, and I'm not supposed to crawl into corner and not live on."

That said, the work I did in counseling also made things worse at times, not better. There were moments I'd be upstairs on the floor of my bedroom with my face buried in a pillow, so that the boys couldn't hear my awful sobbing sounds. There were stretches of time where I came to understand how grounding laying on the floor is. Child's pose was a lifesaver.

Having a professional guide did not automatically solve all mysteries of life and death. My loneliness and sadness got worse—I wanted it to stop, but it wouldn't. In the darkest hours, I really just clung on.

When you become a widow at an early age, it helps to seek out others in your shoes. In the small town of Union, that was nearly impossible; but, in Portland, I had options. For a little while, I was part of a Meetup group for young widows and widowers. A dozen or so of us would go out once a month for dinner. Over chips and salsa or pot stickers and egg rolls, we would let the taboo fly: We would talk of... wait for it... *death*—at the dinner table!

After death, you count these tiny moments of liberation. I was able to mark a few milestones. Okay, I could trust my gut. Okay, wow, I can walk into this restaurant where Dave and I used to eat, and sit and drink a coffee. Okay, death is not taboo. I just cried in front of a.) a stranger, b.) my brother, c.) the boys, or d.) all of the above.

Answer: D!

In this Meetup group, though I didn't want to judge, I couldn't help but compare sometimes. One man told me he still couldn't go near the restaurant where he and his wife had loved to dine—*three years* later. *Wow*, I thought to myself, *that's what being stuck looks like.*

It wasn't right or healthy or kind for me to judge anyone else's grief, I knew that—but in retrospect I can say, that Meetup group just wasn't the one for me. It might have been the only one of its kind back then, but the point is, even if a group is the only one in your area, if your sixth sense is telling you it will not help you move forward, don't beat yourself up for deciding to let it go, let it be, and move on. You do want to learn to filter, of course, doing what feels uncomfortable simply because it hurts versus not doing what feels uncomfortable because it's not a good fit. Boy, I did not want to continue with a crew that, in general, seemed to be having such a hard time moving forward.

Forward was the direction I was heading—and that's when I found Camp Widow.

"Camp Widow?" my brother, Mike, teased me. "That sounds like it'll be a lot of fun—*not.*"

But Camp Widow was outrageously fun. I went in August 2011. We had a dance, we walked or ran a 5K, and most importantly, we were all there because we wanted to do the work—we wanted to move forward with our lives. We did not roast marshmallows, but we did tell ghost stories. We cried and laughed, commiserated and empathized.

In Union, I had had no choice but to be Dave's Widow. There was no escaping everyone's sorrow and pity. I totally understood this sorrow and pity, but there were moments I wished only to live five minutes free of it. I couldn't go to the store for eggs or sit at a sports game without feeling someone's eyes on me.

In Portland, I was granted anonymity, which was a huge relief, but of course, I was digging deeper into doing my grief work. So, although I could go for a walk without worrying about bumping into someone who would remind me of the night Dave died, it wasn't like I could go around celebrating my happiness just yet. I wasn't actually happy just yet. I was walking the baby steps of trusting myself. I was slogging through grief, and that slog was exhausting. In Portland, I never took the five minutes or five hours I might go without thinking about Dave's death for granted; in Portland, I forced myself to get over the guilt of finding it refreshing to walk down streets where not everyone knew my story.

And when I went to Camp Widow, it was all about everyone knowing everyone's stories—and feeling refreshed at the same time! Tears cleanse you and so does instant familiarity: All of us at Camp Widow knew the oddballs we were, or that we could become at the turn of a dime. We knew eggshells and denial, fury and sinking. We knew the worst morning ever.

From the day the boys and I had landed back in Portland in June 2011 until I packed my bags for Camp Widow that August—and for months beyond—I slowly clawed my way out of the numbness. I paid a lot of attention to self-care. Whenever I came across an activity or a "treat or treatment" that might potentially make me feel better—might make me feel *something*—I went for it. If an idea gave me goosebumps, I explored it.

Beyond talking things through with Normina and the usual suspects, I met a woman named Heather Strang. Heather now does work with John of God energy, a healer who works out of Brazil. The queen of spreading healing messages herself, Oprah Winfrey, has traveled to Brazil to meet him. But back when we met, Heather facilitated courses in Portland, where essentially, we learned how to get straight with ourselves and love ourselves before attempting to manifest true love. In private BodyTalk sessions with Heather, I would lie down on a table with a lavender pack over my eyes, and she would work on releasing energy linked to the trauma of losing Dave. Dave came to me in these sessions, always through the left side of my body as goosebumps or chills. Heather and I did past lives work too, and however 'woo woo' it sounds to some, it worked for me when I needed it. It was scary at times, but it opened me up.

In the more traditional yoga and meditation classes I attended, I worked on visualizing a protective shield around me, so that nothing harmful could get to me during my period of intense vulnerability. Learning to ground myself, literally, by going into child's pose while bawling my eyes out into a pillow—or by walking barefoot, had huge benefits. The simple act of having my feet touched during a pedicure did wonders.

Working my way into feeling again required so much more than just a mind over matter effort. Matter *did matter*—my physical body was numb but needy, present but wrecked. Yes, I had friends and family to hug, thankfully—but I knew I needed physical contact beyond that. The loss of physical touch had been so sudden, and though I was nowhere near ready for physical or sexual intimacy, I wanted to feel the strength of a man's hands on me. After over a year of no sexual interest or arousal, I decided it was time to visit SheBop on Mississippi Street in Portland. The staff was amazing. I bought a vibrator, and although it wasn't a man's hands exactly, I named it Sven.

Sven was a godsend, but I still needed real touch. To commemorate our wedding anniversary, I made a special pilgrimage to Bonneville Hot Springs, and asked specifically for a male massage therapist. Dave might have laughed if he knew that instead of getting what I was envisioning—a handsome buff masseuse, a real life Sven—I landed an old potbellied grey-haired guy with a lazy eye. But you know what? It turned out to be just what the doctor ordered: I got a great massage and had a man's hands on me, in a completely safe and professional way. After my massage, I impressed myself by not breaking down entirely. I stayed the night alone, swam in the mineral waters, and went home the next day.

As the numbness gave way to flashes of awareness, and then to deep pain, I also did feel moments of hope. When you are numb, you can't even feel the sunshine. You've got to peel the scab of nothingness away. It's too lonely, walking around like a zombie and telling yourself against all logic that nobody else has ever felt as lost and empty as you have.

Hundreds of thousands of people know grief. I was fortunate to find a whole bunch of these people at Camp Widow. My brother had lovingly teased me about it, but I experienced so many A-HA moments there, and came out of it with a couple of really good friends. In life, you think in general that you feel joy at other people's joy, and you do— but when you see someone from Camp Widow turn their lives around in a way nobody could have possibly imagined at the time, you have no doubt about the potential of the human spirit to thrive. You have no doubt that adversity and agony make us better humans—if we pay attention and do the hard work. You have no doubt that you can somehow get past those nights of whispering into the darkness: "It'd be okay if I didn't wake up tomorrow."

But you do wake up the next morning, and you remember your loss is not a bad dream. You are going to keep waking up to this new aching reality. You are going to feel the urge to stay in bed with the sheets pulled over your head. You are going to whisper more than once into that empty morning light: "The wrong parent died." You will ask when you see a father holding a little boy's hand, "Why Dave? Why not me?"

Evolving isn't just something we do over millions of years, but over millions of minutes. No, I never sunk so low that I wanted to kill myself and I also chose not to go on medication. I knew I needed to feel what I was feeling—numbness is nobody's friend. But I did tell Normina that I thought the wrong parent had died: What did I know about boys and puberty, about sports and locker room talk? What did I know about being a single mother? I needed my partner, damn it.

Normina didn't flinch. She listened and mirrored back to me what I could not see—she reminded me that I was making difficult decisions, I was asking for help, I was showing up daily for Brad and Bryce. She reminded me I had no way of knowing how Dave would have managed had I been the one to go first. He wouldn't have known how to be a mother. Would he have sought professional help? Would he have shown such grace?

I told Normina I was sad. I told her I was pissed. Life was so damn unfair. I was an adult, and okay, it wasn't cool my partner was taken from me, but the boys? Seriously? Hadn't they been through enough? Dave and I used to believe nothing bad could ever happen to Brad and Bryce again. We had worked so hard to assure them they would always have food, shelter, family, friends, laughter, and love. They were safe with us. We weren't going to bail on them. Death is the ultimate bail out though, isn't it?

With Normina's help, I could let it all fly. I became free. I said everything, and nothing phased her. When I got too far out, she stepped in and held that mirror up and prompted me to see what she saw: Stop beating yourself up, Melissa; give up all that you cannot control—essentially, give up control of everything and everyone except for yourself.

After Dave died, I had asked him to put the right people in my path. At the same time, I learned that if I trusted my gut, I could draw those people near—on my own. I could, in fact, live without Dave.

It still stings to say that, but there is no sense denying ourselves the love that does exist beyond a spouse's passing.

CHAPTER SIX

I n the boys' initial paperwork with the Oregon Department of Human Services, Bryce had written that all he wanted was a mom, a dad, and a dog. I would think of the heart-wrenching simplicity of these wants often, after Dave's death.

In all the Kubler-Ross stages of grieving I would go through—when anger hit—I would curse the absolute un-fairness that Brad and Bryce had to lose not one father be-fore they reached adulthood, but two. They'd had six years with Dave. Brad was thirteen when Dave died; Bryce was almost eleven.

I'd had 17 years with Dave and was his forty-four year old widow.

Anyone who has grieved knows that the Kubler-Ross stages of grief—denial, anger, bargaining, depression, and acceptance—are not so cut and dry. In a Psychology 101 kind of way, of course they hold; they make sense; they are guideposts. Before Dave's death, I'd experienced my father's slow demise. I was familiar with grief, but what does "familiar with grief" even mean? Grief is a murky puddle, a hazy abyss, a nerve-shattering test of endurance—it's hard to ever get familiar with something so nebulous and surreal. Grief is a fan of throwing the sucker punch, of delivering your loved one in a dream so real...

Grief is a fan of pulling the rug out again—and again.

I experienced such a different kind of grieving over Dave than I had with my father. After my dad died, my life still went on: I had a partner and a potential family on the way. After Dave died, my entire life as I knew it was over. The movie screen went black. My life would never be the same.

After Dave's death, I dwelled in the denial phase much longer. This probably had something to do with the fact I'd been able to "prepare" for my dad's passing, whereas Dave's sudden death came at me with the force of a thousand stampeding buffalo.

Unexpected deaths are traumatic, and can therefore bring about not only what is referred to as "complicated" grief (as compared to what is called "normal" grief), but also PTSD. According to an article on *suddendeath.org*, "Sudden Bereavement: Responses and Care After a Month," some of the symptoms of traumatic grief are:

- Excessive irritability
- Anger and bitterness, sometimes in sudden bouts
- Continued insomnia and nightmares
- Feeling of unfairness at the death or issues around the death

- Strong feelings of personal responsibility for the death, and/or unfinished business with the person who has died
- A sense that the world as they understood it has been shattered
- Intrusive thoughts about the bereavement, that happen suddenly, when trying to get on with other things
- Difficulty socializing and avoidance of social situations
- Difficulty functioning; difficulty doing daily tasks such as finding it hard to cope with stressful moments at work or stresses when caring for children
- Feelings of futility about the future: What is the point of it all? Disinterest in planning for the future
- These reactions and behaviours lasting more than two months after the bereavement

Furthermore, the article states: "People suffering from traumatic grief are likely to have a strong desire to be reunited with the person who died, and a difficulty accepting the death. They are likely to have intrusive thoughts that revolve around thinking about the person who died all the time, and seeing the person who died everywhere they look... They may also suffer phobias and fears associated with the bereavement, such as not wishing to travel by car if bereaved by a car crash."

The fact I stayed in denial for an unusually long time did not mean I was free of the symptoms listed above. I experienced most of them, to varying degrees, almost immediately. But in my usual fashion, I staved off feeling in

order to get stuff done. "Thanks" to all the moving of resi-
dences and piles of paperwork that needed to be attended
to, and thanks to the boys' sports and school event packed
schedules—I could keep putting many fears and feelings
off. In fact, because of the boys, I had to socialize. I had
to plan for the future, i.e. Move to Portland. Yes, my mom
cooked for us every day for a month and I could hardly eat
what she did cook, but I kept right on robotically functioning while the boys finished their school year in Union.

I grieved differently too, of course, because losing the
person who helped you become an adult is not the same as
losing the person you are being an adult with. Who I was
with my father was sort of a "set deal." Who I was with Dave
was in media res—it was evolving. In hindsight, now, I can
see that maybe I was not evolving with Dave as best as I
could have been—that is—I now know things about myself
I might never have come to know, had I not been forced to
learn them starting the morning I pulled the sheet away
from Dave and realized there was nothing I could do to
bring him back to life.

From that morning on, even in the grip of immediate
guilt and all my "what if" thinking, I went totally numb
and stayed deep in denial. The town of Union had come
and moved me and the boys not once, but twice—and my
mother was with us. She cooked us all those bowls of taste-
less white comfort rice. She attended the boys' sporting
events with me. She ran errands so that I wouldn't have to
spend any more time than was necessary being "the recently widowed, Dave's widow, Widow Opperman," whoever I
was at that time—or rather, whatever I was, because I was
a zombie.

What the hell?!—this was how it felt to be inside my head in those first few weeks and months. *Where is Dave? He's across the state visiting friends in Portland. He's on a long vacation. He's fishing. There's snow and ice on the ground here, but he's not here. He's where it never snows or freezes and he better get back soon. Being a single mom is hard.*

I would wake up those first mornings and close my eyes again—and again. I would picture the fish he'd caught. The photo he'd show me and the boys of that fish—silver and spotted and glistening in the sunlight that was glaring off some lake in the background. How many lakes had Dave and I swum in before we adopted the boys? How many after? The boys and I were buried in this cold—my mom was with us—but Dave was off where fish swam. *Movement. Fish bubbles. Breathing.* Everyone and everything still breathed.

OH NO.

I would open my eyes and close them again. Denial. Hit the reset button—where the hell is the reset button? I couldn't pull those sheets back over my head, even with Mom there. Even if Mom said, "Stay in bed. I've got this covered." No, the boys needed me. The boys needed us. Dave, hurry home. Dave, what the hell?

It didn't really click that he was never ever coming home, until my mom left five weeks later and I had to set the table for three people, not four.

When a dog dies—and Buddy had died in 2008—it hurts to pull that empty bowl off the floor and stuff it away in some dark cabinet corner. When a human dies, it's not pulling the usual number of dishes out of the cabinet that has the power to floor you. At times, I wish I could preach about how we should all truly be grateful each and every time we set a full table. But that's crazy thinking. That's over the top. Oddly enough, you'd live in some terrorized mind space if you let yourself gush with gratitude over every blessed waking moment you have with your loved ones.

My sane mind knew, of course, that Dave was dead. There is no going back once you see your husband's face, colorless. But for months, I was shaking my zombie head constantly: "No, no, no."

Then, "My god, that happened."

My mind clicked like this—denial on, denial off—essentially until we left Union. My mind still clicks every now and again; I still shake my head. In odd and random flashes, Dave's death will hit me. I'll see a dad and a young boy playing at a park together. I'll see my brother-in-law playing with his sons. And I love my brother-in-law and his children—I'm glad for every child out there who has a solid loving parent. But certain gestures or moments will take my breath away for one fast second.

"Oh," I'll think. "*That* was unexpected"—*that pang* of sorrow, or hurt, or even anger. I'll hear a song, or I'll be going through the challenges I go through with Brad, and I'll say out loud: "I can't believe you aren't here, Dave, helping me. I'm doing this alone. Brad wouldn't be battling so many demons if you were still here."

The way the stages of grief are presented, you might think you can work through them in a tidy, logical, timed manner. "Okay, dear therapist, I'll take Denial for six weeks, Anger for eight (yeah, issues!), Bargaining for ten, and so on." I certainly approached Normina that way in our first few meetings when I said to her, like a broken record, "Tell me again how long it'll take until I feel better?"

103

I might as well have asked for the long-range forecast in Portland in May.

Finding Normina and committing to her—committing to doing the work I had to do on myself with her—was my first baby step out of denial. It was me not quite picking the scab and it certainly was not me pulling the scab off in one fell swoop. Entering into therapy in order to move past denial toward acceptance, was me rubbing my hand lightly over the scab, feeling its geography—its boundaries, bubbles, and thickness; it was me believing, wisely, that I was in charge of my own healing and me believing foolishly that I could speed that healing along.

As I began therapy, there were days I would cycle in and out of all five stages of grief within minutes of each other. When anger hit—wow! I was pissed at Dave, then pissed at myself, then pissed at the universe! I would ask why some jackass murderer was still alive, but not Dave. And again, mostly I was pissed for the boys: *They had the dad they wanted, finally.* They had him for sports, leadership, school, barbeques, and snowball fights. But they had him only six years. My anger on their behalf surprised me at times, but I did learn to manage it. Brad would end up taking his anger to a whole other level: he still battles it and maybe always will.

When you start therapy—for grief or for whatever other dozens of deep dark hard reasons there are to seek help— you open Pandora's Box. You can never know quite what you'll find inside your own heart and mind. In fact, the better you think you know yourself, I dare say, the more you'll be surprised at what you don't.

When Dave and I adopted the boys, we were advised not to open their Pandora's Box and we never did find the urge or need to. The boys were young and flexible and totally ready to adapt to a happy family life. We certainly weren't going to probe and delve into their childhood traumas. Firstly, we weren't experts. Secondly, we never wanted them to feel they were different, or difficult, or victims. Thirdly, I guess Dave and I believed that with enough love and guidance, early traumas could be erased, or at least, smoothed over and healed.

Early on, one of the family counselors described part of our job as adoptive parents as "building bridges over the 'holes' left by trauma," and this made sense to us. We were advised to let things unfold however they unfolded, and this seemed like sound advice. We realized the boys would always carry "stuff" from their past—much of it tougher than anything Dave and I had experienced in our youth, but some of it universal. So their "stuff" would always be with them, but we would always be with them too.

The way the boys' trauma and pain manifested after Dave's death—Brad turned toward anger and Bryce regressed—must have stemmed from what happened and did not happen in the years before we found each other. And I know that for young men especially, there is still such stigma attached to admitting, first, a need for help, and second, actually getting it. Dave, Brad, Bryce, and I had learned how to build bridges together as a new family, but I am also now a pretty hardcore believer in the notion that everyone can benefit from some form of counseling or coaching — whatever age, whatever gender, whatever the trigger.

I needed some counseling after Dave's death, and not just for his death.

I've said I had a happy, fairly uneventful and conventional middle class upbringing, and it's true. But not many of us manage to come into adulthood whole and wholly amazing. Our flaws and patterns, our desires and needs and pet peeves, just *are*. I had always imagined I was in control of who I was and what went on around me, but the work I was doing taught me that I had to let go of so much more than the guilt I felt over Dave dying. I had to pull out parts of myself that weren't exactly the shiniest prettiest parts, and I had to reframe or discard them.

When your partner dies suddenly, or rather, when my partner died suddenly, I lost all confidence. Maybe this is typical, maybe not. Maybe the friends of mine who I consider the most calm, cool, and collected, would be that way under any and all circumstances, even death—*even sudden death*. I envy them that, but I also know that after Dave's death, I needed to cut myself a huge break if I wanted to move out of the numbness, denial, sadness, and anger. I needed *to break* into even smaller pieces than I already had. Losing Dave shook up my entire life, including my sense of self. Dave and I had always functioned as a team, and then one day I woke up and my team was gone. Everything I knew was turned upside down.

As I was rebuilding, in those early months of weekly therapy, I'd rollercoaster from feeling completely pissed to totally weepy, and I wouldn't understand why. Tapping into feelings I had never had to go to before was no walk in the park. Feelings, when you sit with them, run the gamut— you've got your soft fuzzy feel-good feelings, and you've got your cold sharp-edged steamrolling and bludgeoning ones. Most of the time, you go along in life doing your thing and most days, you get in touch mainly with those feel-good feelings: How are you? You *are* fine, despite the typical daily annoyance or challenge or two.

In grief counseling, I was not fine. I felt like an open wound—one that remained open, exposed, and vulnerable long after I exited Normina's office. For days on end, I was a raw nerve, and this was very uncomfortable for me. In Union, I'd felt at times that everyone was looking at me: I was "Widow Opperman." But even in my liberating anonymous days in Portland, in my toughest therapy weeks, I felt there too like everyone was looking at me, seeing right through me, and judging me. Nobody was, but because I was opening up and entering completely new territory—— some days it was hard to see and to believe that I was doing okay. How could it be true that I was doing the best I could, if for the first time in my adult life, I was crying wherever and whenever I felt like it? I had never let people see me cry in the past. Now, here I was in Portland, letting it all hang out.

In our most intense transitions, we are often feeling so much so deeply, we have no clue where we will land. This is probably why people stop short of major breakthroughs, or why they quit therapy in the early going—self-work is grueling. It is all on you! With a great therapist, you get support, but you must also hold yourself accountable. You cannot run and you cannot hide.

Not only was I in denial about Dave's death (even though I knew it was a fact of life), but I was in denial about myself: "I do not have control issues."

("Okay, so how can I ensure the boys won't die in their sleep. Okay, but I have to wake up every hour on the hour now throughout the night to check that they are breathing. Okay, but if they sniffle, I must take them to the doctor—Yes, I do mean immediately!")

I even tried to control, at first, what I shared with Normina. It took a couple months to trust her with my innermost craziest thoughts, and it took almost two years for me to let go of my hypervigilant habits. Writing this book six years later, PTSD would hit. But the more I trusted the process, the more I would confess, and the more I could begin to let go.

"Do the work," she would always say.

And I did treat getting to know myself like a job.

"I understand why you feel compelled to check on the boys every night. You lost Dave in his sleep. But Melissa, you have no control over how anyone lives or dies—none of us do."

All we do have control over is how we react. Even now when I feel out of control, I will start to worry about myself or people I love, dying or being harmed—and then I will work on what I can do with this worry.

You can't control people by worrying about them. Ruminating is a waste of precious energy. I try to stay aware of my thoughts: Oh, what an interesting thought! But I do not judge them. Most thoughts we have are not real things— they never manifest. Learning to let go of all I could not control—which was essentially almost everything—freed me to tap more into my feelings than I ever had before. Being able to identify my feelings is a gift I received out of loss.

Yes, it has been hard for me to verbalize the notion that anything positive could come from such trauma, but the truth is, Dave's death *eventually* was not all sadness. For better or worse, I have learned some incredibly useful things that have changed my core being and my life in a positive way.

Dave and I were good partners; we were best friends. What I learned and gained in our long relationship affected in a positive way my relationship with my future husband, the man I am married to now, Sean. We all bring issues and tools to the table, but I knew what partnership had looked like, and I knew what I wanted any future version of it to be. I knew, despite the small voice inside me that was saying: "But you don't want anyone to die on you again, Melissa!" that I wanted to have a partner in life again. Thanks to the work I had done on myself, my vision about having a significant other—and more importantly, my vision about being a significant other—had evolved. I had evolved.

When Dave and I got married, we said: "Let's just go for it," and we stumbled, rather happily, along. With Sean, right off the bat, I was more verbal. I'm more honest with Sean than I ever was with Dave, because I'm more honest with myself. I don't mean, of course, I ever told lies to Dave, but that I speak my truth about how different experiences make me feel. I rarely did that with Dave. We had a great partnership, and I never compare, but knowing myself better has made everything I do, *different.*

Doing the work and going through parenting and my life alone for a couple years helped me move into my own self and inhabit that space. I said: "Okay, yes! I'm putting myself first. I'm getting my needs met first, because if I don't, then I won't be able to be the best parent I can be. I will speak up! (Oh, wow, this is uncomfortable for me!)"

But I did it. I took up space and I spoke while I stood there.

This wasn't as simple as it sounds. I didn't put on my Wonder Woman cape and boots and belt and start flying around punching bad guys in the nose and flirting with Superman. Like I said, much of the time I was gaining strength, I felt weaker than ever. I don't understand the physics of that to this day, but I don't question it—plenty of books and proverbs and poems have been written about finding our light in the darkest spaces. All I do know about the physics of acquiring self-knowledge, is that it requires a lot of physical self-care, and while I did go through a period where I treated myself and my body to yoga, massage, and Body Talk sessions, I also mistreated myself and my body some too.

Immediately after Dave's death, wine, beer, and cigarettes tasted horrible to me. I've written here that for the first month he was gone, I mostly subsisted on the white rice my mother cooked, and applesauce. But a year or so after Dave's death, I'd find myself gravitating at night toward a beer or a glass of wine. Sometimes I would join a friend for a pint—that's what living in Portland is all about, after all. But often enough, I would drink alone, and at a certain point, one glass of wine would turn into an entire bottle—or more.

Around this time, after making sure the boys were asleep downstairs, I'd grab my wine, listen to music on earbuds, reminisce or cry, then take a little toke of weed. I'd never been a big pot smoker, and I'd thrown out most of Dave's stash, according to his wishes. But I had kept some, as I mentioned, in the little fleece bag we had bought together in Joseph, Oregon. I had kept his little wooden pipe, because his lips had touched it. So I'd drink, smoke, and zone out. I'd think: *Maybe I can talk to you this way, Dave; maybe you'll come to me tonight.*

Needless to say, drinking and smoking alone did not mesh with my investments in self-care. I'd be hungover at work, feel bad, then repeat myself again the next night. I was irritable with the boys; I was not on my A-game. A pattern was forming, and I could see it, so I went to my brother, Mike, who is in recovery and hasn't had a drink in fifteen years. "So, this is what I'm doing," I told him. "What do you think?"

"I think you've been through a lot and this is your way of coping. I don't think you're an alcoholic, but this definitely sounds like binge drinking, and it's something to pay attention to."

Drinking had helped me sleep—I would pass out. Smoking pot had helped me imagine I might be able to talk to Dave again—but in truth, I found him when my mind and body were clear, not hazy.

I went to my brother for a reality check, and without hesitation, he gave it to me. Immediately, I mellowed out. I'm still a social drinker, but I'm vigilant. In challenging times of the year—winter, for example—I'll cut back on my intake, knowing that alcohol only temporarily keeps pain and difficult truths at bay.

Throughout all my more effective "methods and experiments" in facing the pain and truth—*Dave was gone and he was never coming back*—I spent hours burying my face in my pillow, weeping. Buzzed or sober, after a fairly decent day of exercise and yoga, or after a horribly lonely day with a tub of ice cream, tears were never too far. I just don't think there's any way around crying buckets.

As any pet owner knows, animals are incredibly good at catching our tears. Buxton was no exception—he offered up eighty-five pounds of pure love and was a huge part of my healing. Our dog was always there for me, sleeping with me every night, and licking my hand when I cried.

But Buxton suffered the sudden loss of Dave too. In Union, he had always slept between us at the foot of the bed. When Dave used to come home at the end of the day with the boys, Buxton would bound out of the front door, tail wagging, mouth open in an ridiculous toothy grin. When I'd come home in Dave's truck—with no Dave—the look on his face was one I could only describe as disappointed.

The move to Portland took a toll on Buxton too. Moving from six acres to roam to a fenced yard—and again, still missing Dave—he became anxious. He began losing his fur. He had been so loyal and strong for the boys and me that I decided he needed some support too: We took him to the Portland Humane Society for group dog "social work". I cried there too—I'm telling you, both suffering and healing could cause a sudden outburst—but eventually we worked our sweet boy back to a healthier state. Buxton follows me around the house now like a shadow—he follows Sean too.

Dave's death forced me to face all kinds of truths—from the practical, "My god, why didn't we write a will and testament, this paperwork is hell!" to the deeply emotional—we all missed him so much—to the physical—I would never be held by him again.

I also learned in my grieving journey, that speaking my truth—standing up for myself—wasn't something I had practiced often, with anybody, including Dave. What did that mean? In working things through, I came to realize that I had almost expected Dave to know what my truth was. Now I know it wasn't fair to think he would read my mind, but in retrospect, I can see that the times I did speak up, it didn't really work for our dynamic. I didn't feel heard. I could say to Normina, "He is not here for me to talk about this with now, but I'm not sure he was there for me to talk about this kind of thing then, either."

When I said this, it was a huge revelation. It was freeing, enlightening, and a little sad.

So what were friends and family experiencing during this Becoming Melissa project? I don't really recall any specific observations others made about my changes and decisions—at least not until issues with Brad came to a critical head, and I had to make the hardest choices a parent has to make. But even then, because of the work I'd done to get through my grief and to get to know myself better, when I was making decisions that people thought were a little drastic, I knew how to stand in my truth and say: "I love you, but I don't want to hear your opinions."

Standing in your truth and starting with the words, "I love you," works. It is amazing. Trust me: People, for the most part, will understand. Nobody, or practically nobody you know of, will say, "You're being a real bitch these days."

And who cares if they do? They aren't in your shoes and don't know what you know.

❧

The boys and I had moved to Portland in June 2011, six months after Dave died. I started working with Normina in July. I would go back to work in the office, with my same company in the Portland office, that fall—though Dick would be gone and I would begin to show signs of unravelling by late winter, and would give notice to quit that spring. I'd start nursing school pre-reqs. I'd reimagine myself.

But before all the deepest hardest breaking down and building up would come, in August of 2011, I'd attend Camp Widow.

While I was still in Union, desperately scouring the Web for grief resources and guidance, I stumbled across the Soaring Spirits Loss Foundation website and Camp Widow. They were holding one in San Diego at the end of summer, so I signed up. I went on my birthday. I did not want to celebrate my birthday that year.

"What are you going to do at Camp Widow?" my brother Mike teased. "Sit around a campfire and cry?"

"No, smart-ass," I said. "It's at the Marriott."

Of course, I had no idea what to expect. Would we melt s'mores over those little butane stoves they use at wedding buffets? Would we flood the Marriott lobby with our tears, or move through the corridors like harbingers of doom?

I have to say, it is hard to carry doom in southern California, when the sun is shining. Camp Widow was super refreshing, and surreal. Literally hundreds of widows descended upon San Diego! All of us wore badges around our necks indicating our names and "how far out" we were. When I saw a veteran, I'd seek them out.

And one poor hotel guest—he joined a group of us in the elevator at a moment we just all happened to be laughing our asses off. He glanced at our badges.

"Camp Widow? Hmm," he said.

Widows could laugh? What about? Hmm, indeed! When the doors opened and our confused companion hurried out, we laughed even harder.

One woman I spoke to, Cassie, is still a friend. She was not a veteran. Her husband had also been named Dave: he had also been a teacher, and he had also died suddenly (six months after my Dave did). Cassie was ten years younger than me and had no children. She and I buddied around. We went to different seminars; we attended cocktail hour. Over drinks, everyone openly asked: How did your husband die?

It was the first place I'd been where nobody was afraid to talk openly and at length about death. Nobody treated you like you were going to break. We listened to each other's stories. We cried and laughed and some women had stories more horrifying than ours. What? How was that possible? The experience was so freeing.

There were so many people like me.

Some of the more far out widows seemed to be thriving, and some were not; but, we all wrapped arms around each other. It was a beautiful three-day weekend of learning, processing, and yes, even dancing! A dance that is made up of 95% women is freeing in itself. Of course, it was held at the Marriott and any male guests could have walked right up onto that floor and worked their magic—but contrary to the Hollywood version of "post-death hooking up syndrome," something about the rumor "All of those women have dead husbands," kept us safe. We couldn't have been more content.

I considered registering again for camp in 2012, but decided not to. Maybe some of us only have to have that door opened once—that liberating confirmation that we are not alone and that love lives on. Maybe I will go again at some point—I don't know.

I will always carry with me the most precious lessons I learned throughout the grieving process. I will likely always learn new lessons about grieving. Never ever fool yourself that you are prepared for the next death. Never fool yourself you can prevent it either—with worry or with love.

I'm no counselor, but when a colleague loses a spouse, if it seems appropriate, I'll offer a "to-do" list. I offer an ear and a heart too, of course, but I know all too well that when your spouse dies young or unexpectedly, practical help and practical steps are crucial. Dave had no will. You hear from time to time stories about what levels of pain and hell having no will cause, right? Yes, right. Plan now, prepare now—save your loved ones that extra agony.

If you cannot take the time or don't have the resources to spend a few days at Camp Widow, or to get extensive grief counseling, find books and one good friend. Know that you are not alone. Thousands of people are feeling exactly what you are feeling at this very second—they're feeling the good, the bad, and the ugly. They're feeling the guilt too—I could have, I should have... or even, I want to be married and happy again—what the hell kind of betrayal is that?

But the truth is, life does go on. Impossible to believe at first—an almost repulsive fact you want to reject and be blind to—the world doesn't stop when your best friend, lover, spouse, or child passes. I remember well walking through the grocery store in La Grande, watching everyone go about their business and wanting to scream: "What are you doing people? Don't you know my husband died!"

I could have gotten stuck on the "life isn't fair" train easily, but I knew I couldn't let that happen. Life is not fair, but life is a gift, and there are more gifts for you to discover, possess, and then share. You won't want life to go on at first, but eventually you'll see life is not the best listener.

CHAPTER SEVEN

Neither Dave nor I had ever probed too deeply into *why* Brad and Bryce and their siblings had gotten what seemed an unfair deal in terms of their early childhoods. We never wanted to put down their biological family; we never wanted to make them feel "odd" for having been fostered and adopted—or like victims—because they weren't any of these things. When the boys came into our lives, they were more or less simply ready for love, play, friendship, security, and guidance. We provided all of that to the best of our abilities.

Dave, Brad, Bryce, and I made a super tight family unit. We were living on Mount Emily. Dave was well respected at the school and the boys were playing sports, getting good grades, and making friends. I was realizing working from home all the time wasn't for me, but for the most part, I was living the kind of life I'd always lived: comfortable, fun, and active. If my main complaint was about my work life and I sometimes wished I could clone myself in order to be a better mother, hey, I chalk that up as pretty normal.

Only after Dave died and I was cycling in and out of sadness, numbness, loneliness, despair, anger, disbelief, fear, and craziness, did I ask myself why the boys had been dealt so much, so early in their lives. Bryce had still been in diapers, at age five, when we adopted him. Nobody had taken the time to deal with the basic elements of care and upbringing for this little boy—in all of his moving about, adults and the system had failed him.

I would ruminate: *Who loses two fathers in such a short timespan? Why?*

I would come to accept, that dwelling on these kinds of thoughts was useless. There is no satisfactory answer to the questions: Why is life unfair? Why do the innocent suffer?

Stuff happens is the basic answer—and no, it isn't a satisfactory one; and no, I don't mean it to sound as blasé as "shit happens." But the truth is, stuff does happen and some of us sail through it, some of us work our way through it claw and nail, and some of us barely make it to the other side.

The boys and I were devastated by Dave's death, but while Bryce and I would find our way through, Brad would need significant outside help. The hardest decision I would ever have to make in my life would come after Brad's therapist in Portland said: "He is shut down. I can't help Brad, Melissa. It's a waste not only of your money, but of everyone's time."

I bawled when I heard these words. They came a year or so after we'd left Eastern Oregon, and the situation with Brad had been worsening, but I still never expected to hear a professional "helper" admit to feeling helpless. And this guy was great, which made his admission all the more troubling.

From the summer of 2011 to the fall of 2012, the boys and I had had a year where it almost felt we were "chilling." I had quit my job in the summer of 2012, in order to dedicate myself to healing and parenting. When Dave's one-year death anniversary came around, I had been about to crack. Normina was my weekly anchor, and she helped me to understand that my most important task was to feel my feelings and work through cycling through numbness and pain so that I could emerge stronger and more whole.

I returned to school in 2012 to fulfill pre-requisite coursework for nursing school. I was envisioning going into hospice care and leaving finance and contracts behind. These were my months of practicing extreme self-care. I drove the boys to school, then went to my school—Portland Community College. I studied, I meditated, I got massages, the boys came home, we ate dinner, and sometimes I cried myself to sleep.

But for the most part, that first year home in Portland, though we were all mourning Dave's death, we were also moving through it —until Brad couldn't.

Looking back now, I feel I was given that "chill" year in order to get my shit together, because something awful was about to go down. I had no idea mid-chill how stressful things would become, but thankfully I had that fairly uneventful year to fortify myself.

The boys had never been fans of talk therapy, and I didn't force it, but in late 2012, when Brad started to have trouble at school—he was at Central Catholic—I took him for a few chats with Normina. She saw the cracks too; she told me she was "very concerned."

During our Portland chill year, as I said, I felt the strongest and the weakest I ever had. I was learning how to be Wonder Woman, while weeping in public places. The whole time though, I knew that I was fortunate, especially as a young widow and mother of two boys, in being able to afford to quit a job to explore another career path. I felt proud, excited, and refreshed. I was beginning to believe too, that even though I felt overwhelmed by single parenting, I was a pretty good mother.

Oh boy. Beware those flashes of pure confidence. Beware the calm before the storm.

I thought the boys were marching through their grief fairly well. They had always been resilient, more resilient than I had ever had to be in my youth—and so, I kept the faith. They could see how much I loved them; they could see that although we'd lost Dave, we had not lost his love.

It started to become a couple weeks into Brad's sophomore year at Central Catholic that things were not as they seemed. He had just turned fifteen, when I got a call from the Dean of Students. Brad was accused of being involved in a physical altercation with another student at the bus stop. He denied it, or rather, he minimized it (saying something to the effect of: "My hand touched his face."). Central Catholic, understandably, suspended him. When he returned, he showed disrespect to a couple female teachers.

Basically, Brad's entire sophomore year, I felt like I was on the Dean's speed dial: Brad was blaming others, he was not taking accountability, his homework was going downhill—nothing was getting better. At home too, things

121

were escalating: There were holes in his bedroom wall from where he had thrown trophies, batteries, and who knows what. My entire family was concerned.

I got Brad a therapist, but early on the therapist told me: "It's like child abuse, forcing him to talk when he doesn't want to." Brad had never been a talker, even with Dave. They had been close, but Brad wasn't the type to warm up entirely to anyone. This concerned me. I wanted so much more for him. I wanted him to be and to feel connected.

Central Catholic knew our story and they were very tolerant. Nevertheless, the Dean told me that at the end of the year they'd hold a panel to discuss Brad's future at the school. This panel expelled him, with the caveat that if he worked through his issues over the summer, he could possibly return. We all knew what was at stake and tensions at home were maxing out, but I kept the faith that summer. Brad was calling me terrible names, rolling his eyes, and even bumping into me on purpose; he was threatening too, I would later find out, Bryce.

That summer, I put Brad into Outward Bound in Colorado, one that specializes in teens who have experienced the loss of a parent.

I knew Brad was in pain and that there was rage, but I was also in the process of grieving and healing, and I had to protect myself. I had to protect Bryce. I had to save my family. Dave was not there to do it for us. While Brad climbed a mountain in Colorado, Bryce and I hung out with friends in Denver and Boulder. Brad then came home and worked as a counselor-in-training at a local summer camp in Portland—he was great with kids. At his hearing at Central Catholic that August, they granted him permission to return for his junior year. I breathed a sigh of relief, but just one... because then things escalated at home. All of Brad's negative energy turned toward me and Bryce.

It was at this time Brad's counselor said, "I'm sorry, I can't do anything more."

"What would you do?" I cried. "What would you do if this was your kid?"

"It will be expensive."

I had money. I had Dave's PERS retirement money. I would spend most of it over the next two years, for the sake of my family.

***

Educational Connections has branches in Oregon, Washington, and California. Drs. Patricia Phelan and Ann Locke Davidson founded the organization in 2001, and have extensive ties to experts and therapeutic programs that specialize in helping at-risk youth and families connect, heal, and thrive. Most people come to them when traditional routes have failed. I came to them at this point, for Brad.

The therapeutic programs do not come cheap—and even though Brad and I still struggle at times to speak the same language, I don't regret spending the money I spent. This was Dave's retirement and pension, and frankly, I think he'd be pissed if I hadn't used it to keep Brad from falling over the edge and ruining his chances to have a great life. Brad is in college now and he's living independently, but without Pat and Ann and the teams of amazing people those two women led us to, I can't say for sure what would have happened.

The loss of Dave had been devastating, but figuring out what was best for Brad was one of the scariest times of my life. I felt completely unsure of his future, but simultaneously totally sure I had to do something about it. Trusting my gut during this chaotic time meant wrestling away some of the issues I had with letting go—but ultimately I managed to get my son the kind of help that I was not equipped to provide.

Pat and Ann worked up a full evaluation of Brad, based on a series of interviews. They interviewed me, of course, and members of my family. They interviewed people at Central Catholic. Everyone knows that Brad is smart, funny, athletic, and capable of intense focus. They know too, he is a courageous survivor. Not everyone agreed with me when I decided, via Pat and Ann's guidance, to send him to a therapeutic wilderness program in Central Oregon for 13 weeks. We had survived cold on Mount Emily, of course. But the kind of cold he would be going to, in the tent he would be staying in, would truly be a "wake-up call" kind of cold.

This is what I hoped would crack Brad open. We all knew that another of Brad's "strengths" was his ability to keep stuffing pain in. In some early evaluations at wilderness camp, it would be reported that staff counselors were expecting Brad to explode.

※ ⊹ ⊹ ※

I wrote letters to Brad the whole time he was away. "I'm feeling overwhelmed," I would write, "and I need you to step up and work with the counselors there." I had given him so many chances, but in the two weeks prior to scheduling his "late night pick up" for wilderness camp, I had brought all the golf clubs from the basement up into my room. I don't admit this lightly—it took months of therapy with parents just as afraid and full of shame for not being "good enough" at parenting—to understand just how many parents are afraid of their kids. Right now, one of your neighbors is suffering in silence, I guarantee it.

I was scared. I was worried. I didn't want my family to be this way. I wanted Brad to treat people well, build strong connections, and become a successful adult. I was a single mother trying to raise a boy whose hormones were raging on top of complex traumatic emotions he could not handle unless he "ignored" them.

As adults, we think we know what ignoring emotions or the truth results in. But even as adults, like I've said, we mostly sail along until something hard and awful happens, and only then do we wake up and take a deep long self-assessment. After Dave died, I can't tell you the number of people I think must have asked themselves: *Am I truly happy here and now? Where exactly am I? What have I been doing with my life and how have I been living it? Do I love the person I'm married to? If I were to die tomorrow, would I be semi-okay with that? Or what?!*

Brad was full of anger, and a great portion of it was directed at women. Maybe because his birth mother let him go, maybe he sees all women as weak? I don't know. He has never said this to me, or to anyone else, as far as I know. It's just a guess.

But I did get reports from wilderness camp over the thirteen weeks he was there, and I know the place was a solid first step for him.

How do all of these parents who are literally at wits' end, force their angry, troubled, self-harming, defiant teenagers to take this first step?

We don't force them. There are professionals who do the driving, literally, for us. It cuts through the emotion. It offers no out for the child in distress. It is one of the scariest things you will do as a parent, and possibly one of the greatest reliefs you will ever experience.

I gave Brad NO advance notice that he was going away. I hired two men—referred to me of course, through Educational Connections—to pick him up and drive him to the wilderness program. It is in my nature to take care of business, so I did. I spent hours when the boys were at school and I was between classes, interviewing teams of people who would hopefully help lift my son out from behind all the walls he had built. His fortifications were strong—he had been at the construction game since he was a very young boy. Had Dave stayed alive, maybe the process of crumbling those walls would have continued and there would only be a few bricks to trip on.

We will never know.

But on Thursday, November 14, 2013, I prepared. The pick-up team would arrive at 4:00 a.m. on the 15th. I sent Bryce to spend the night at my friend's house, odd for a school night, but my friend knew what was going on. I stayed up all night. I reviewed what the pick-up team company had told me: "The day before: Pack ten pairs of underwear, we'll take care of the rest. The day of: You'll come into Brad's room with us. You'll introduce us. You'll tell him we're good people and we are not going to hurt him. You can say a few things, and then leave the house. You will leave the house before we do. We'll lock up."

When I saw the car pull up, I went outside and signed a few documents. One of the guys was named Leo, which I took as a positive sign: My dad's name was Leo. I turned the light on in Brad's room. I spoke as calmly as I could, although my heart was pounding so hard I thought Leo and his partner could hear it.

"Brad," I said, "as you know, things aren't going well, so you're going to a wilderness program. Right now. Do you understand?"

Brad pulled the blankets over his head.

Leo asked him to pull the blankets away. They shook hands and introduced themselves. "Your mom is going to leave the house now, Brad. Hit the bathroom, and we'll get some more clothes together."

I left the house and went to Mike and Erin's house. They had coffee ready and waiting for me.

Leo called ten minutes later and every hour from the road. At that point, I gave up all control.

It was the scariest thing I'd ever done, but I was resolute about something needing to change.

⊱⊰

Brad went to New Vision Wilderness in Bend, Oregon, for thirteen weeks. Given the intensity of his grief—and the even greater force of his efforts to conceal it—I was aware those thirteen weeks would probably not be enough. Pat and Ann had seen hundreds of young people and teenagers go through multiple programs, back-to-back. Recidivism for at-risk kids is high. The purpose of all of these amazing programs is to try to catch everyone early enough, so that back-sliding doesn't become an issue in terms of say, cycling in and out of jail.

Still, I felt sad and guilty. I'd sent Brad away right before Thanksgiving and Christmas. The Thanksgiving and Christmas prior, had been our second without Dave. The holidays are still painful for me. I imagine it's still painful for Brad. Bryce, I think he was young enough still to escape all the roughest associations. After several weeks in the program, Brad and I had began weekly phone therapy—he was out there in the cold, and there I was trying to work things out with him and a therapist. These sessions were rough, but the family therapy visit weeks later would be brutal.

When I had picked up Bryce from school on November 15th, he knew something was up. He'd been shadowing another student at Central Catholic and had texted me: *Brad's not here today.* I had texted back a fib: *He's not feeling well.* When I did tell Bryce the truth, I could see he was shocked at first, but then he was relieved. Over the next few weeks, he would tell me he'd been taking a lot more heat from Brad than I knew. Poor kid. Had he been trying to protect me—knowing how much I had on my own plate in missing Dave? Had he been fearful of ratting his brother out? Had he been trying to prove to Brad how strong he could be too, after the death of another dad?

Only after Brad was away did I realize how tense things had been for all of us—Bryce included. I can't say it was wonderful to come home to a house with one empty bedroom, but it was a very necessary relief. Bryce needed my attention. He had taken a backseat, and now I'd have time to check in. He was having some troubles at school; we would right them.

※━━※

In January 2014, three years after Dave's death, I was gearing up to tell Brad he was not coming home straight after wilderness camp. In fact, he'd be going further away, for a longer period of time.

Bend was having one of their coldest winters ever, but Bryce and I headed down for our first family therapy session.

I had been getting progress reports all along—hearing that although Brad remained guarded, he had cried more than once about missing Dave. He was able to say now that he missed his father. He was able to move beyond moving— that is, he could open up just slightly without having to loosen up a bit first by tossing a ball or running down a basketball court. For the first time, he could actually acknowledge his pain. When I first heard he had cried, I was happy.

I cried happy tears because there was more than anger in my son. In my gut and mind, I had known this, but it had been so long since I had seen a tear or a vulnerable moment, that I had begun to wonder if it was possible to entirely cut feelings off. Feelings sucked—I knew that! But the alternative would be horrific.

Brad ran toward us when we arrived. He hugged us. He was happy to see us. None of this behavior was behavior I took for granted; it was so nice.

We built a fire with the therapist, Ricky, and we talked for two or three hours about how losing Dave had affected us individually, and as a family. Then, Ricky pulled me aside and said: "It's time to tell Brad he's going to a long-term program. Use as few words as possible."

I hadn't decided yet on which program I was going to send Brad to—I'd been debating between Discovery Ranch in Utah, and Boys Town in Nebraska. Still, I managed to choke out something like: "Brad, you're doing great work and we miss you but you need to continue on. You're not coming home yet."

I purposefully did not say to Brad, at this point, "I love you." I didn't want him to hear, "I love you, *but…*" I didn't want an association between loving and shitty news to somehow form in his mind.

"Why?" he asked. "I'm doing really well here. How will I be able to prove to you I've changed?"

This was the first time I had seen Brad cry in a long time. It brought me to my knees.

I was sobbing. Bryce was sitting there. Ricky was trying to facilitate, but what could he do? He knows there is nothing harder for a parent than to see their kid broken down. Of course, the point of wilderness camp is to break them down—and you trust these professionals and they are your last damn resort—but man, did we all get quiet. The woods we were in got sad and quiet. The four of us sat staring into the fire until Ricky said, "Time to put it out."

The boys and I and Ricky walked back up to camp through the cold. I thought of our last winter on Mount Emily. Brad was walking ahead of me, looking back to make sure I was there. We hugged and parted.

⊷⊰⊱⊶

At this point, Sean and I had been dating for about a year. We'd met each other's families and things were getting serious. I wonder now if Sean's family thought then: "Who the hell are you dating? Her son is where, exactly?"

I'm sure some of my friends and family worried about me sending my kid off to the woods in the freezing cold, and then telling them, "And next he'll be going to Boys Town. And, um, living with a bunch of other troubled teens in a family situation."

What the hell?!

But at some point, and again I kept looking forward. I told myself, "Nobody is in my shoes right now. This is hard as hell, but this is right for me and my family."

It was so hard. If I had been working at that time, I would've needed wilderness therapy too.

Why does wilderness camp therapy work for some, and why does it not quite work enough for others? I learned so much throughout the entire process—from Pat and Ann at Educational Connections, from the counselors at camp, from the interviews and eventual meetings I would have with the people at Boys Town. Everyone in my parents' support group had kids who had gone to wilderness camp. The theory is you get your kid totally out of their element—you shock the system. But here in the Oregon wilderness, kids who were in trouble, shut down, addicted to drugs, gaming, booze, sex, you name it, experienced a total cut. The cold and the hiking and the building shelters and the chopping wood weakens your almighty child. And from there, you hope, therapists can "sneak in" and do some work getting them to their emotions. Interestingly enough, a lot of the kids of the parents in my parent group were adopted.

Brad graduated from wilderness camp. A bunch of us drove to Bend for the ceremony, and then my brother Mike and I flew him directly to Omaha. You are instructed not to take your child home. They do not visit friends. In February, after wilderness camp graduation, we drove straight to PDX, barely making the plane due to snow. The next morning, we were at Boys Town in Omaha.

Did Brad trust me and my decisions at this point? I have no idea. But I did.

I had flown to Omaha two weeks prior to check things out. A couple days later, I'd missed my flight to Utah, which seemed a further sign that Boys Town was the right choice. I had met the family Brad would live with, and they were amazing. Chris and Lori were a married couple with two kids of their own, who had been doing the Boys Town Family Home Program for twenty-five years. They have since become good friends. Bryce and I flew out when Brad was six weeks into the program, for part of Spring Break. In addition to my weekly calls with Brad, Chris, and Lori, I would visit every couple months.

I still felt like Brad's mom, but I had also given up some control. For fourteen months, Brad lived with his family in Boys Town. He graduated from Boys Town High School, and in addition to getting the Buffett Scholarship to Nebraska, he received a Boys Town scholarship and several grants.

Is Brad still mad at me for sending him away? I don't know. Years of therapeutic living does not erase years of pain.

Learning and practicing cognitive behavioral therapy and going from being "defensive" and disrespectful to capable of saying you miss the man who wanted to guide you through manhood, does not translate directly into "healed, better, perfect, cured."

My relationship with Brad is still not a bed of roses, but it isn't the "highly emotionally charged" relationship it was when I sent him away to Bend.

I would love for us to have a conversation one day about Dave's death and the events and experiences that followed, even if I'm eighty years old—not because I am expecting an apology, but only because I know talk brings people closer. All I've wanted the whole time I've been Brad and Bryce's mother, is closeness. It is what I like to offer.

I don't need to hear the words *I'm sorry*. I want Brad to take accountability for his actions, but I also understand that much of the time he was—or is—raging, it is not him, it is a sheer inability to control the enormity of the pressure.

The nature-nurture discussion is relevant—Brad had an entirely different life before Dave and I came into it— but each foster and adoptive case is so different. Book upon book upon book has been written regarding attachment and its various malignant forms—same for dissociative behaviors, ADHD, ADD, PTSD, and all the "boy ailments." We devour these resources and when they aren't enough, we reach out to therapists. When therapy doesn't help, where do we turn? If we have funds, we are lucky. I knew parents who sold or took out second mortgages on their homes so that their children could attend wilderness camp, or Boys Town, or, like Brad, both.

I took Dave's retirement money and did what—*I had decided*—needed to be done.

We do our best. And by we, I mean biological moms and dads, adoptive moms and dads, and our children.

CHAPTER EIGHT

I know I'm not the only widow who has talked to her dead spouse and who has wondered: *Would he understand if I just laid in bed all day—for two days straight? Is he watching me undress right now? What would he do if another guy leaned in to kiss me?*

I'm probably not the only widow either who has experienced the sinking feeling of not really knowing what her departed spouse would have wanted or expected of her, *as his widow*. Would Dave have wanted the boys and me to move through our grief as quickly as possible? He had always been a proponent of picking oneself up by the proverbial bootstraps and moving forward if something wasn't working out—if something was making you unhappy. He never did believe much in depression.

But you know, at that point, I didn't care what Dave would have wanted or done. I was still mad at him for leaving us. No, he had no control over his death, but I had no control over feeling angry about it either. Logic and grief rarely walk hand-in-hand.

Clearly, it wasn't Dave's spirit force that propelled me to take care of business—that's what I had always done and again, that's what the boys needed, so I did it. Besides, even though Dave's friends and I had talked about finding those garage windows at the Mt. Emily house mysteriously open after being closed, and though I'd sensed and smelled Dave so keenly on that early morning walk in Union when I was finalizing my decision about Portland, I wasn't sure I believed—entirely—that he could or would perform any physical act beyond a little trick with a window.

Maybe he just wanted to breathe our air again.

I know many of us have thought about how our deceased spouses might give us a sign they're still with us—will they move a coin up and down a door right in front of our eyes, maybe? We saw *Ghost*. We saw how Patrick Swayze (rest in peace) had to learn to use his anger to move things. And we saw what angered him: Another man—his murderer, yes, but basically, *another man* who wanted his partner, Demi Moore.

Another man?

Demi couldn't, I couldn't, who could?

For months and months, the possibility of ever meeting anyone else never even entered my mind. To entertain the idea of liking or loving or marrying someone else—what? No way! It was me and the boys, period. I was still in love with my husband. I had taken off my wedding ring, but not to signal I was single.

What I could do and did do in setting out a new life course, after almost breaking down entirely and quitting my job, was focus on being a mom and going back to college.

I loved being there for the boys after school. I reveled in the opportunity to be the kind of mom who had dinner ready and has unlimited time to help her kids with their homework. And as a "mature female student," I felt right at home taking my pre-nursing coursework at Portland Community College. Thousands of adult and non-traditional learners attend PCC, and I never felt awkward there. At first, I did worry about my "old" brain's capacity to process new information, and math was a real struggle because I hadn't used it since high school. But I loved the experience of being on campus; I loved to be able to say, "I'm doing this!"

I had quit my job, I was raising two boys on my own, and I felt at home—in the city, in my city, Portland. No lake I had ever jumped into in Eastern Oregon had ever felt so exhilarating. I threw myself in completely.

At PCC I battled algebra, wrote papers for English, and took yoga, tap dancing, and pilates. I took psych classes too—studying those oh-so-well-outlined stressor scales and stages of grief—but viewing them now, of course, with a totally fresh perspective.

I valued my college days at PCC and did all the work. After dropping the boys at school in the morning, off I went to my own hallways and classrooms and semi-healthy cafeteria lunches. I did my homework at the college library too, so that after school, I could be a 100% full-time mom. Again, I was fortunate to have been in the financial situation I was in. Not all widows can quit a job—nervous breakdown pending, or not. Not all widows can afford to go back to college.

I took nothing for granted. I was still also battling my fears and destructive tendencies, especially at night: *Are*

Brad and Bryce breathing? Now that I'm able to cry openly in front of people, will I ever be able to stop? Will I make a good hospice nurse; will I comfort people?

Nights, all the worries that couldn't catch me during daylight hours did. Things with Brad were beginning to go off the rails at this time too. So, I'd have these days—busy and interesting and full, full of promise—and then I would get those phone calls from the school. I wasn't kidding when I said I felt I was on Central Catholic's speed dial at one point. Brad was acting up and out on an increasingly regular basis. Had I been still working at that time, I'm sure I would have shattered.

⚊⚬⚊

I completed most of my nursing pre-requisites, and fully planned to focus on end-of-life and palliative care—I figured I'd be adept at assisting people and their families through the grieving process. I wasn't through it myself, but, I knew what kind of work had to be done. I knew the challenges of the work intimately. I would have been a good nurse, I'm sure, but in the end, it was too difficult to get into a nursing program, and with all that was happening with Brad, I let the nursing idea go. It was for the best, my heart wasn't in it and I was excited to be open to other opportunities.

I focused on taking care of Brad from a distance, and on taking care of Bryce—who had so very much needed the break from his brother. And yes, I decided to start to date.

Brad was still living at home when Sean and I first met. I can't say if part of his troubles were associated with me

moving forward, and in his eyes, trying to "replace" Dave—
which of course I wasn't. But either way, Brad wasn't happy.
Bryce on the other hand instantly liked Sean—he has always bonded fast with father figures.

Bryce had always been easy going. Sure, in the earliest
days of living with us, he had his fears: Would we run out
of food? Were the doors locked? Would they be forced back
into the foster care system? But when Brad did leave for wilderness camp in Bend and then for Boys Town in Nebraska,
I was able to see clearly just how tense and stressful our
living conditions at home had become. With the house in
Portland to ourselves, as hard as it is to say it out loud, Bryce
and I were able to breathe better.

As the weeks moved on, with Brad in Bend, slowly the
stories began to spill forth. While the usual, brotherly,
rough play had been going on in the year following Dave's
death, it came out that Brad had threatened Bryce physically more than once. Worried about whatever else Bryce
had been holding in, and with his grades dropping slightly
for the first time ever, I had him do a session or two with
Normina alone. His pediatrician did a depression screen-
ing and a general checkup, and came up with a diagnosis of
situational depression with a Vitamin D deficiency—110%
normal for a young Pacific Northwest boy who had recently
lost his father.

I kept an eye on Bryce, relaying this information to his
teachers, and working to get him back on track. All the energy I'd been focusing on Brad, all those months, I could
now spend on Bryce. When I think about how he kept all his
troubles to himself for so long, I feel bad. Was he doing it
to prove to his brother how tough he was? Was he thinking,

"I better not add anymore to Mom's plate?" My go-with-the-flow kid had always been flexible and rarely showed agitation, but as a parent, you still want to check in with the one(s) who aren't making waves. Ask: Are you really taking this death as well as you seem to be taking it? Is there anything you need to tell me? Is there anything more I could be doing for you?

Bryce came to Dave and I a very empathetic and caring child; he is now an empathetic and caring young man. When I started dating Sean, he took that in stride too.

⇥⊩⊩⇤

When we first moved back to Portland, two of my girlfriends stepped into high gear to support me. My friend Colleen became my Saturday night date. Even though she was married with children and working, and I was single with children and going to school—we managed to go out on the town every once in awhile and whoop it up. It kept us sane. We checked out new bars and restaurants—and in Portland, I swear one hundred new places must open every month now. We danced at old stomping grounds and didn't care at new stomping grounds that we were the oldest women there.

We did Eighties nights—where we could almost always count on hearing Dave's band's classic cover, Brick House.

Colleen was the girlfriend that suggested, when I first started talking about the possibility of entering the dating scene again, that I get braces. She works in the dental industry still, and it's a "fix" that automatically comes to her mind.

"Yes!" I said. "Just what middle-aged me needs as I take my position in the singles playing field again. Ha ha!"

I got the braces. They were no big deal.

At the same time, my Ya Ya friend Jane said, "If you're going to start dating again, you've got to make a list."

"A list?"

"Basically," she told me, "You sit alone and drink a couple glasses of wine. Write down everything you want in your next partnership. Be really crazy and really deep, but just write. Don't judge or self-censor."

I had been with Dave for seventeen years. I had been in a very solid partnership. I knew what love looked like, and knew its challenges. I knew I had grown. My list of what I wanted in a new partnership came out to almost four pages.

I did drink a few glasses of wine and listed what might be considered simple and shallow things: *Must be taller than me, and a good speller.* But I also went deep:

1. Has to have good relationship with his family.
2. Must be comfortable with me talking about Dave.
3. Has to respect my parenting style.

Sean easily hit over 80% of my list, and in truth, as I've gotten to know him, he probably hits closer to 90% now. You don't run from numbers like that. You count on them.

The first time I met Sean wasn't actually the first time I had met him. We came to learn, very early on, that we'd run in the same circles since we were children. We'd gone to Catechism together in grade school. We'd graduated from the same high school, the same year. Surely, we'd shopped at the same food store, because for a few years, we lived on the same street, a few blocks apart. I used to walk Buddy by Sean's house.

I didn't tell Sean right away either, when we were discovering all of this weird proximity stuff, what that first psychic I went to had said to me. I mean, at first, it really didn't even click, because what that first psychic had said had honestly been too much at the time. I had broken down in tears and put her messages out of my mind.

This was the psychic my very Catholic mother had recommended. The one a friend of hers had sworn by, after she'd lost her son. "He was there," my mom's friend had told her. "And there was no way this woman could have known what she knew."

Still, I went as a skeptic. I went as a blank slate. I gave this psychic no information before visiting or up front, when I sat down at her table.

In that session, my father and my grandmother came to me first. Then, Buddy, our old black lab. "This black dog's body is spread out between you and some strong male energy. Did somebody die? Did your husband die? Was he a musician?"

Dave came through midway. After the psychic relayed the message that Dave was touching his heart, or his chest area, and then pointing to his head, as if to say he had died from a blood clot or maybe a lung embolism—again, something I will never be able to confirm, but which felt accurate to me, she said: "Dave wants me to tell you that he has something to say to you that you might not want to hear."

Oh, great. This session was taking place during my "period of intense and open crying." I braced myself, but at the same time, stayed completely open. I wanted to hear Dave.

Dave wanted to tell me I was going to meet someone. He had picked him out for me. This man was going to be my love—I would meet him the following summer—he would be an engineer. The psychic said, "Dave loves you and wants you to be happy."

"Also," she said, "your boys will be fine, despite some rough patches."

I of course sobbed, and then put it all on the furthest back burner.

I did tell Sean about the psychic much later. Sean is a software engineer. We met that next year, in early September, so technically, in the summer.

Prior to meeting him though, I had done some "pre-dating practice" with my friend Joli. I had to. After so many years with Dave, I had no idea if I could hold an intelligent or interesting conversation with total male strangers. How did I decide to overcome this fear—this fear of making an ass of myself? Speed dating.

Speed dating was all the rage at the time and it terrified me, so I decided: I have nothing to lose. And what to gain? Really, I didn't care. I don't think I went to the Speed Dating sessions to find a date; honestly, I just wanted to dip my toe in the water. The water was funny and a bit weird. In one session, nobody over age forty-five was supposed to be there, but one man clearly had snuck in. "So," I asked, "where'd you go to high school? ... Oh, and what year did you graduate? ... Wait, 1964? ... Haha, no worries. I won't tell."

Then there was the guy both Joli and I took an interest in. He ended up calling me, but he also ended up refusing to meet me in public. "Just come over to my place and we'll watch a movie," he kept insisting. Nope. Weird. Possibly dangerous.

Joli and I did no more speed dating after that—not necessarily because of that bad apple, but because I had decided to move on to MeetUps. Here, it seemed I would have a better chance of meeting likeminded people, in settings that interested me. I'd get to do all of this too, in real time.

I met Sean on my second MeetUp, which was one he'd organized. It was for single parents between the ages of thirty-five and forty-five, and twelve of us met at the fabulous Portland restaurant, Noble Rot. After our "meet the chef" chat and rooftop garden tour, we all sat down for a wine flight and cheese board. When I overheard Sean mention that he'd gone to Tigard High School, I turned from the person I'd been talking to and asked him, "What year did you graduate?" (This time, even though I wasn't quite sure of Sean's age and he did have silver hair, I wasn't trying to trick him into admitting he had snuck into the wrong MeetUp.)

He'd graduated the same year as me. What? He knew my brothers, they were in the same choir together and had travelled to Europe when they were kids. Whoa. We'd been in that Catechism class together in third grade. But Sean and I had only vague memories of each other. We left Noble Rot exchanging emails, and then weeks went by where we exchanged a few friendly, but non-committal, emails.

"He's got to ask me out," I thought. "I'm going back into this dating scene and the man is going to ask me, the woman, come hell or high water."

A week or two went by, and I said, "Oh well," then I said yes to what I thought was going to be another intimate MeetUp wine tasting event in SE Portland.

This MeetUp was no gathering of twelve though. I walked in and there were probably one hundred people. I was alone, and I almost turned around, but there Sean was, waving at me. He bought me a glass of wine, but right when we started to chat, I spotted someone I knew, so we separated. Again, he'd had my email and had sat on it for weeks, so I figured he wasn't interested. When I saw him getting ready to leave twenty minutes later, "Hey!" I said. I walked over to him, "Sorry, I didn't mean to ditch you."

Sean didn't leave. That's when we discovered not only had we gone to the same schools, but had lived on the same street. He had been head of the soccer association Brad and Bryce played in. I had passed his house, with our dog. Finally, I broke my "woman new on the dating scene" rule and said, "Let's go do something fun together."

Sean said yes.

Brad was in his downward spiral when Sean and I started dating. That couldn't have been easy for Sean to witness. Of course, he had his own share of single divorced parent issues. Neither of us came to the dating scene with veiled eyes and fuzzy illusions. When I ended up sending Brad away, first to wilderness therapy and then to Boys Town, I wondered what his friends and family might have thought of me. But then, that was the time period too where I was beginning to truly own my own decisions and stand firm in them. So, I wouldn't say I didn't care what anyone thought of me, but—I guess I didn't. I was proud of having come so far; I was determined to do what was best for my children. Bend and then Boys Town was best for Brad. I believe that to this day.

In those weeks and months prior to sending him away, there'd been so much anger in our home that nothing else could come through—not from any of us. After he left, and I heard from his therapists that he was hurt, crying, and grieving, I felt shitty, but I also felt relieved. Though in my rational mind I had always known Brad was in pain after Dave's death, anger had taken up so much space, and hurt us all so deeply, that my rational brain was too exhausted to remember "pain underlies it all; pain is the reason." The anger was so harsh; I had to protect myself. I was losing weight again at this time, and not sleeping.

With the force of the anger removed, Bryce and I were able to breathe again. I was able to gain better insight into my parenting style. Parenting had been such a conscious choice for Dave and I; we'd thought all of it through so seriously when we filled out those adoption forms. We'd managed so well together. And then it was just me.

I still say I speak Russian and Brad speaks Chinese. We have very different ways of communicating. Sean has said once or twice, "Can you speak more dude to him?" But I'm not built that way. That's not how I talk. And Sean respects my parenting style.

⚔

Eight hours—that's how long my first date was with Sean. By this stage in my post-Dave life, I had had glimmers of happiness. I had done things that I'd never done in my pre-Dave life—things that had scared the hell out of me, like speed dating, like going back to school, like being a single mother. Doing these scary things made me feel like I was running a marathon. And you know—marathons are grueling, but afterwards you realize how amazing you are and how amazing you can be.

Do scary things when you're grieving; do scary things when you're already feeling alive. Glimmers of happiness turn into extended periods of good times and even, bliss. Good times turn into major breakthroughs, accomplishments, and opportunities to make definitive life choices.

Sean and I started out on our first date having dinner on SE Clinton, and we never ran out of things to talk about. We moseyed over to PokPok, which of course, was packed; so, then we headed to a bar across the street. At one point, Sean's sister-in-law called, asking him to meet up with them in their neighborhood. He hadn't told them that he was out on a date, but asked if I'd like to go "meet his family."

"Ummm. I don't know. That seems like a lot right now."

Awhile later, we ended up heading over to where his family had been, why not? But they were gone. There may have been one awkward moment then: Okay, now what?

Sean broke it with: "Let me show you my favorite park."

"Your favorite park, huh? I bet you say that to all the girls?"

I gave him shit about it then, and I still do sometimes.

The view was great, but of course, it's the kiss I remember. Sean was polite about it.

"I'd really like to kiss you," he said.

"Okay," I said, in a nervous-as-hell but super-happy Melissa don't say *I thought you'd never ask* kind of way.

Action! Two adults are kissing like teenagers in a parked car, in the dark, at Sellwood Park. The leaves have started to fall, but not enough to reveal the sparkling Portland cityscape. Who cares? The adults have other things to do.

"That was my first kiss," I said.

"With braces?" Sean asked.

I smiled. Oh my god. I was fourteen-year old Melissa again. I was a version of me I didn't fully know yet, but was actually beginning to love: young me and wiser me, with some of all I'd learned in between and through parenting and grief me.

"That was my first kiss since Dave," I said.

And basically, Sean and I said nothing; we both felt, "Whoa."

CHAPTER NINE

When you start dating someone you have unknowingly been crossing paths with for decades—someone you could have easily bumped into a dozen times and thought nothing of, had he been at his mailbox in his slippers and robe while you strolled past with your dog and a pocketful of doggie poo bags—you do wonder about chance and fate, close calls, and things that were meant to be. Top that off with a psychic telling you that your departed husband supports your happiness with another love, and you really might begin to question how thin the line is between not just life and death, but also one life path or another.

It wasn't as if I kept what that psychic told me on the front burner: *This man is going to be your love— he will be an engineer and Dave is fine with all of it.* No, I hadn't been ready to hear those words when I first heard them a year after Dave's death, and I wasn't chanting them and crossing my fingers and lighting candles around any online dating site or Meet Up shrines many months later when I did decide to give dating a try. Even after writing that very long list of traits I wanted in a future partner, I was making no conscious effort to find the man Dave's spirit supposedly was telling me it was okay to find.

When I set out to date again, it was a half-hearted adventure, a task almost, a testing of the waters. I wasn't testing men or love or what the word "forever" could mean—there is no forever; I was testing myself.

I had lost my husband, my life partner; I was raising the boys my husband and I had adopted, solo; I had quit a solid familiar job and gone back to college; and I'd worked intensively on myself. I was allowing myself to cry, alone and in front of people; I was allowing myself to say "no" and to express what I wanted; and I was learning to ask for help instead of feigning that I was cool, had everything under control, and could handle it all by myself. For months and months, I had been moving toward everything I feared most and loosening my self-imposed chains of control and self-discipline, so why not see if I could actually put on some lipstick, walk into a restaurant, talk to a man, and be intrigued and intriguing?

Maybe the challenge was even less significant than that: Could I be comfortable in my own skin and have fun with someone who was not Dave, my husband, my life partner who was no longer alive?

When I met Sean at those first two Meet Ups, he was dipping his toes in the dating waters too after a self-imposed dating hiatus. Having gotten divorced roughly five years prior, he had been in the dating scene longer than I had, but for his own reasons, was hesitant about trusting too fast too soon. On our ridiculously fun and familiar eight-hour first date, though he'd spontaneously asked, "Do you want to meet brothers and sisters over in Sellwood?" (which didn't happen), we did not meet each other's children until a full six months later—and sisters and brothers and parents came after that. Intimately, we took our time too. We had both been in long-term committed marriages before and knew what we wanted: One of the things we wanted was to take things slow and easy.

In some ways, dating each other turned us both into teenagers again: I mean, our first kiss *did* take place while I was wearing braces, and despite all the initial positive signs and giddy feelings, we were both unsure. For whatever reason, I mean, I am not particularly old-fashioned, I was stuck in the mind space: *He needs to keep calling me if he's interested. That's just what I want a man to do right now.*

For that entire first month, Sean and I were participating in an awkward teenager-esque dance of hesitancy. All those decades circling each other, we had had our near misses, and at that second Meet Up, Sean had almost left early after I said a very quick *hello, thank you for the glass of wine, I see a friend.* Even with a couple of fun easygoing dates under our belts, neither of us was assertively pursuing the other. Me, again, I was determined the man should call; Sean, I can't say, but maybe he was more worried about my status as a widow than he could admit, maybe he wanted to give me wide berth and didn't want to pressure me. I don't know, but I do know that the day after Thanksgiving, I was feeling anxious about the touch-and-go of it all. Sean had suggested we do something after Thanksgiving, but I thought, "*Something?* That's vague.

And *after Thanksgiving?* That could be before Christmas or after New Year's Eve!"

So after a delicious Thanksgiving meal at my brother's house, my niece, who was in her early twenties at the time, said, "I hear you're dating someone," and then, "Why don't you call him?"

"Yes," I told her. "I'm dating someone. I mean, I think I'm dating someone. I'm kind of dating this guy, Sean. He's great. But I have no idea what's going on."

"What!? He's great? Text him right now, Aunty Mel, and suggest going out. I do it all the time, you can too."

I wasn't much of a texter, so my niece, who clearly knew how to date better than I did, helped me construct the perfect text message. Sean responded within two minutes: *Let's do something tomorrow.*

⚓

That next day, Brad and Bryce stayed with my brother. It was a cool crisp bright sunny day, and Sean and I took advantage of it by visiting different spots around Portland. We started at the top of a building downtown, cruised through Mt. Tabor Park and sat at an overlook, drank beer here and there, ate crepes in Northwest, and made out. Basically, we made out in Northwest, Northeast, Southwest, and Southeast Portland, and from that day on referred to that date as the Portland Make Out Tour Date, and also as the date when we knew we were going to go for it, come what may.

From Date One, to the Portland Make Out Tour Date, to now, Sean and I have always talked a lot, like teenagers— yeah, we talk *a whole lot.* From the start, we also played a lot, as if the city of Portland were completely new to us, as if we hadn't lived forever knowing the Mississippi District, food carts on Hawthorne, Powell's Bookstore, 23rd Avenue, the Veritable Quandary (VQs, now gone), and Crystal Ballroom. Of course, Portland is always new, for the past decade in particular it has been growing like mad; but when Sean and I weren't out listening to music or dancing in some venue neither of us had ever been to, we were talking. When we weren't stuffing our faces or sipping wine at some fabulous new Portland restaurant, we were talking.

One thing that intrigued me about Sean from the start is that he wanted me to talk about Dave. He asked questions about Dave, and then listened to my answers. He *held space* for me, before that phrase even came into popular mainstream consciousness.

Outside of therapy, situations involving close family and friends, and special places such as Camp Widow, most people are uncomfortable hearing about people who have died. Of course, they ask: "What happened?" or "How are you doing?" or "How are the boys?" or "How can I help?" But for the most part, talking about death or the dead in any meaningful way puts everyone on eggshells or brings everyone instantly down, which is crazy and disheartening, because we are all guaranteed to die and to lose someone we love or cherish.

Yet, after someone dies, it is often the burden of the deceased's spouse or close family members to put the rest of the world at ease. I had become used to people, upon hearing me speak the word "widow," shutting down. I would find myself saying, "Sorry," when the fact that my husband had died suddenly and young in our bed stopped people in their tracks, made words impossible. When possible, I would avoid questions or situations that were guaranteed to lead up to a discussion about fathers—or more specifically, to Brad and Bryce's fathers. I would do the same with the topic of husbands—mine, Dave; and the same with the topic of death—Dave's, cause unknown; and with marriage and widowhood—my forever cut short, "I'm so sorry."

But of course, in trying to avoid all of those topics, you realize how often they come up on a daily basis. I heard "I'm so sorry," and other general niceties and genuine condolences, but Sean's openness to hearing *more* about Dave was not the norm.

Sean's interest and openness was not *abnormal* either, though at first, I found myself glossing things over. I had dug so deep into Dave's death with my own research of grief, and I had made genuine huge healing strides, but I still was not 100% ready to share elements of the life I'd led with Dave, with a new man. I found myself walking the line of being appreciative and somewhat in awe of Sean's willingness and desire to hear about my "previous" life and not be intimidated or uncomfortable—and my own questioning: How much is appropriate to share? How close to the core can I get to the relationship I had without betraying it, and without withholding from this new relationship I am building? How can I honor Dave and our marriage? How can I hold space and time in my heart for both men—which I did, which I still do, and which Sean has always accepted?

I had done a lot of work on following my gut: I was learning to care less what was considered appropriate, or "the norm," in regards to grief and its timelines and cycles, but when you are falling for someone new after realizing how much pain can be attached to love, your gut is in a bit of a whirl.

I had gone through many new experiences since Dave's death, and had for the most part, grown and succeeded through them all, but love again? How was it possible? And what had Sean and I learned from these partners we'd had prior? What did we want to carry forth, and what did we want not to repeat? I don't think I was processing all of these questions at the time, but I certainly hadn't read up on "how to love another man after the heartbreak and trauma of losing the one you thought you'd be with forever," because loving another man again hadn't been my goal—not so soon, anyway.

I'm not a fan of the clichés "expect it when you're least expecting," and "love finds you when you aren't looking for it," but I have to say, some clichés ring true. No, I wasn't dating willy-nilly or painting the town red like some wild happy child in a candy store, I was still very much focused on healing and on making sure Brad and Bryce were okay. Testing the dating waters was meant mainly to be part of my healing journey, but then there Sean was, immediately—as if someone had put him in my path.

During this time, Normina had been suggesting I should probably "keep dating a little bit." It's the advice most of us give or receive after losing or leaving a long-term love: Play the field, don't settle down again too soon, keep testing those waters! It would be this advice from Normina, in fact, that would start me down a path that was independent from her. I had worked with her so extensively for so long, and I was beginning to feel it was time—I had the tools to work through tough decisions on my own for awhile now;

I knew how to eventually find my truth and speak it. I was doing so with Brad and his worsening situation at school and at home; and I was doing so with Sean. Plus, although nobody said anything directly, except Normina, I knew in my gut that staying single and shopping around wasn't for me. More importantly, I knew that I didn't have to explain or justify not wanting to play the field to anyone—I did not have to follow any post-spousal death falling in love again rulebook. Sean and I not only had endless things to talk about, but we also spoke the same language.

In addition to wanting to know more about Dave, Sean had questions about the boys we had adopted. Again, his questions were the normal kinds of questions one single parent asks another—but at the time, Brad was spiraling into deeper trouble and it was important for me to remain undeterred and strong in terms of moving forward with what was best for him. Not that Sean questioned any of my choices in regards to sending Brad to wilderness camp or to Boys Town, he was not, in fact, involved in any of that particular decision-making process, but in general, while I was figuring out, "Is this man going to stick?" I kept him at arm's length in relation to the boys.

⤛┼┼⤜

At about the half-year mark, Sean and I knew our relationship was going somewhere, but we still postponed any heavy duty "family-blending activities." We had met each other's kids, but we kept most of those meetings brief. Sean was a gamer, so he would chat with the boys about gaming when he came to pick me up. His older kids were living on their own, and his daughter, Jasmine, was usually out and about whenever I came around, so for the most part, we continued the focus on us as a couple.

So then, here's a truth for widows and non-widows, widowers and non-widowers: You cannot help but compare the people you date, love, or marry. You are told you shouldn't; you try not to; you might not verbalize most of your comparisons; your comparisons may be major or minor or both—but you do it, I do it, we all do.

Dave and I had always been music lovers, but for the most part, we saw the same bands, including his, of course, when he played. We visited our familiar haunts and didn't often venture past them. Sean's taste in music was more eclectic, and together, we branched out some. Sean organized the thousands of songs he downloaded in ways Dave didn't: *brutal death metal* versus *death metal* (don't ask me!).

Sean was a planner, whereas Dave never had been, except for when he taught and coached. Planning vacations with Dave, I always made the hotel reservations and nailed the itinerary details down; Sean and I plan our travels and vacations together, and ultimately, I've discovered I like that. I also like Sean's romantic side—he picks out flowers for me for no reason at all.

Of course, it isn't important really, how a man organizes his music collection, and I did made travel arrangements when I was with Dave without much of a fight. I love getting flowers now, but never realized I was missing them that much before. Dave and I worked very well together as a couple and we knew which battles to pick. One thing you know though, if you've lost somebody you love, is that you cannot always know *when* to pick those battles. After someone dies, you never forget the last battle or moment of friction you had—no matter how familiar or seemingly insignificant it was.

On Mt. Emily, I had been growing increasingly stressed in the months prior to Dave's death. Even though I knew we would be moving into town the next school year, I couldn't help but feel impatient. That snow and ice; that digging out of our cars and power outages and working from home and feeling isolated, it was really tough on me. It is hard to say out loud, but that December, right before Dave died, we were both frustrated with each other. We weren't exactly fighting, but I remember he got me a blender for Christmas. "A blender?" I said. "Don't you know me?"

I was the one who would go out of my way to find that special guitar pick Dave had mentioned over toast and eggs three months prior. I was the best stocking stuffer in town. But I knew Dave: He had told me plenty of times he wasn't a huge fan of Christmas. He thought it was overrated; said there was too much pressure. The fact that he gave me a blender that Christmas didn't surprise me, I think I was just at wits' end in that house.

There are differences between the two men I married, naturally; but more importantly, I am a different woman. Dave's death shook my foundation—it cracked me to the core. From those cracks, some of the old Melissa escaped, oozed out, and fled. Sometimes the process of emptying myself and transforming was ugly, frightening, shocking, and completely beyond my control. Sometimes, I felt like a carnival balloon somebody had popped. Other times, I purged old ideas, fears, and beliefs on purpose, and after-wards felt a thousand pounds lighter.

I wouldn't say I *let go and let God,* because religion never did help me through Dave's death; but I sure did learn to *let go and let be.* In his well-known hit "Anthem," Leonard Cohen sings: "there is a crack in everything, that's how the light gets in," and in many ways, I can't think of a better line for those who are grieving. I tried for months not to acknowledge my cracks, or I attempted to cover and numb them. But into those cracks, a whole lot of new life and new Melissa entered.

I was never a dark or angry or depressed person be-fore Dave died, and everyone who knows me would verify that claim, but even the most carefree and generally pos-itive-thinking person can benefit from more introspec-tion. I don't wish it on anyone, but there is nothing like the death of a loved one to spur on deep questions about the meaning of life and what you'll be doing with yours, as short or as long as it is meant to be. Working on your-self at any time, has value. Working through your fears or weaknesses at any time, fortifies you. We're all vulner-able, but we're also capable of becoming more whole by claiming that vulnerability—by standing there and stat-ing from time to time: Damn, I guess I'm not superhu-man after all.

The Japanese art of Kintsugi consists of pouring a gold, silver, or platinum dusted lacquer where ceramic vessels have cracked, which rather than hiding damage, illuminates it. Christy Bartlett, the author of *Flickwerk: The Aesthetics of Mended Japanese Ceramics,* writes: "The vicissitudes of exis-tence over time, to which all humans are susceptible, could not be clearer than in the breaks, the knocks, and the shat-tering to which ceramic ware too is subject."

Whatever it is that shatters us, and whatever state we are in prior to the events that shatter us, we can heal in ways that make us even more beautiful, or in ways that make the light that was always meant to shine through, shine even brighter. It isn't easy to say or to hear, but death can bring gifts. We are going to lose our loved ones and we are going to suffer—there is no avoiding the feral pain of grief; we can honor the depth of that love and loss by recovering and maintaining our resilience.

⚔️

Even after Sean and I decided we were going for it, and even though we were crazy about each other, neither one of us thought we would remarry. The issue was, we were spending so much time together, and it was a drag coordinating across two opposite sides of town—like I said, Portland's growth in the past decade has been outrageous, traffic is hell!

The logistics of dating—are you serious? The economics of dating, right? Two households—is that really necessary? In August of 2014, we moved in together. Bryce was going to a private school, so we could live anywhere. Brad was at Boys Town. And Jasmine, Sean's youngest daughter, lived with us too. Each of us had to work out some stuff in those initial weeks and months, nobody manages the Brady Bunch like the Brady Bunch did. But soon we were in the flow, and soon, Sean proposed.

It's funny that Sean, the amazing planner that he is, proposed the way he did. He still says, "It didn't quite come out the way I wanted." We still laugh about it. We had been with our friends on the Oregon Coast, and Sean said, "We should go shopping when we get back to Portland."

"What?" I said, "Like grocery shopping?"

"No," he blurted out. "Ring shopping!"

Yes, the proposal was not in line with Sean's usual M.O. He is the guy who not only offers flowers at every right occasion, but offers the right kind of flowers. But "Yes" is what I said. Yes, to the logical and scientific engineer a psychic told me I would love. Yes, to the guy who doesn't get too annoyed when my controlling side pops back up: "Are you sure you did this, Sean; are you sure you checked that?" Yes, to the guy who cannot spell even though "Must be a good speller" was on that long list of qualities I was looking for in my next life partner. Yes, to Sean, the brutal death metal loving man I make text me every time he rides his bike to work because yes, I still worry more than most people that I will lose the people I love way too soon.

⊱⊰

While Sean and I were planning our wedding, sure, once in awhile I questioned: Is it too soon? I believe most widows and widowers cannot help but ask themselves this question—well, unless they've been serial daters or serial spouses before. Sean and I met almost two years after Dave's death: Was that enough time? I went to books and to websites looking for answers, but then I remembered that I had to forget what others did. What was right for others was not necessarily right for me. *This feels right, this feels good*—I was ready.

I knew what felt right and good, not only because I'd had right and good with Dave, but because in the two years following his death, I had experimented and tried so many new things and had learned the art of self-care—I knew myself better than ever.

Sean and I got married on June 27th, 2015 at the site of our first overnight outing: McMenamin's Gearhart. June 26th was a cold and windy day and June 28th, it poured down rain. The day we said our vows, in the shortest and sweetest ceremony ever (it was 7.5 minutes long), the weather was gorgeous.

With my father gone, Sean and I decided we would walk down the aisle together—nobody gave me away. My sister-in-law, Erin, got ordained and married us. Brad DJ'ed the dance party.

Dave's sister Nina was there with her family. After the wedding ceremony, when everyone was drinking beer and noshing, she and I shared a moment together. "I'm so happy for you," she said, hugging me. We held each other. It was the only time I cried at my wedding.

There are days I feel like I have two husbands: I still talk to Dave and refer to him as my husband. Dave is not an ex-husband, not a former spouse. He is my husband, or my husband who died—but again, there is no good way to say it. Sometimes Sean tells me that it feels like there are three people in our marriage, and I don't deny it—sometimes there is. I don't know if I would be as gracious and accepting of "the love before me" as Sean has been since we first started dating, but deep down in his engineer's heart, I think he knows we were meant to be because he knows life doesn't always work by "either: or" principles.

CHAPTER TEN

Before I even considered going to a Meet Up, before bringing anyone else into my life, I wanted to be sure I was good with *me*.

I'm not talking about "love yourself first so that you can be loved:" I had loved myself *enough*, years back, before I married Dave. And besides, I'm not entirely convinced everyone who has partnered up successfully waited until they fully knew or loved themselves. Clichés, right? Some of them ring truer than others. Imperfect and hardly-self-aware people get together and make it work all the time. And I know that nobody is perfect, but I was more self-aware than ever—and I just wanted to stock the odds more in my favor the second time around.

When Sean and I first started dating, I was definitely still healing, but I was also feeling solid and grounded. Counseling, self-care, and the support of my friends and family got me through the roughest patches after Dave died.

I got me through the roughest patches as well. I had been rolling along slightly frustrated, but mostly fine, when life threw me that widow curveball; I was broken wide open; and then I grew stronger. Before dating again, basically I didn't mind being that Kintsugi bowl, I just wanted to be sure all the cracks were sealed—that I still could hold everything.

In the early days with Sean, I had my moments of doubt—about him, about me, about us as a couple, about blending our families, about second chances, life, death, you know, all the small stuff. But seriously, for the most part, we put each other at ease and laughed our asses off. Dating Sean felt good. And who doesn't have doubts about dating, especially dating over age forty after a long-term relationship has "ended"?

A year or so into being together, Sean and I had ironed lots out in terms of who we had been in our previous marriages, who we had been as single adults and as single parents, and who we could and would be together and as stepparents. For the first time in years, I was feeling calm, secure, and happy on a regular basis. Yes, anxiety reared its ugly head from time to time: I'll probably always carry the trauma-induced fear that everyone I love will simply stop breathing one night. If I wake up in the middle of the night I always check to see if Sean is breathing. This fear—the one that is least likely, but also obviously very possible—may never go away. Fine, I'll live with it.

Guilt, in many ways, has been harder to live with than fear, or even sadness. My fear that I'll lose everyone overnight is ludicrous, I know; and my sadness regarding Dave's death now, for the most part, is tinged with sweetness. I am grateful for what we had. The guilt though, likes to cling—and it shapeshifts. Rarely now do I visit those awful "what ifs" of those first few hours and weeks and months post-losing-Dave: I have come to terms with the fact that there was probably nothing I could have done to save him that night. Had I been in bed with him, gave him CPR and called 911, whatever took him probably did so before paramedics could have arrived.

That damn house on the mountain.

But one thing that guilted me when I first started dating Sean and first began to realize he was a potential life partner, was the boys. They hardly said a thing about our relationship—they didn't try to make me feel bad, nobody did. But I found myself needing to explain to Brad and Bryce several times: "Hey, I'm dating, but you know I loved and miss your dad, right?"

You say these words and they hear these words, but you never quite know if they believe you.

What you can do when guilt comes knocking like this at your door, trying to drag you across the threshold—and down? Stand up to it: Take a deep breath and make an honest assessment, and then stand in your truth. *It's okay. Stay true. Everyone will be okay.*

My boys could see I had done the best I could after Dave died. They knew what kind of mother I was with Dave, and without him. Even sending Brad to wilderness camp and Boys Town was my way of showing the boys I was willing to do whatever it took to keep our family healthy and strong. In easy times and in crisis, I don't think my boys ever doubted the amount of love I had for them. Even sending Brad away, which in itself was guilt-inducing, I had to step back and give myself credit: I had done so much research and so much communicating and networking on his behalf. I had quit my job to heal and explore other career paths, but mainly, I quit to be a full-time mom—to make sure the boys and I got through the death of this teacher, musician, and coach we had all loved more than anything.

The truth I stood in when I started to fall for Sean was this: Here is a great man who is wonderful to me and who will be wonderful with the boys. That's all I needed. Was it too soon for me? No. Was it too soon for the boys? I may never really know. Did I know how to live with never really knowing? I sure as hell did.

But again, part of the work I had done on myself after Dave's death entailed putting my own needs before others, at times. In order to survive so that I could be the strong mom and woman I needed to be, I learned to explore and declare what my needs were, and then to go for them, despite any questioning (imagined, usually) or push back (rare, for the most part) from others. Did people worry about me? Did people talk about me sending my son out into the woods or then out of state for assistance in raising him? Did they think I should keep playing the field?

A few of my dearest friends and family members might have been concerned, at times. There may have been whispers of doubts here and there, but for the most part, I found that the more confidently I stood in my own needs and motivations, the more my friends and family were able to see that I really knew what I was doing. In the middle of the hardest days and nights, I admit that sometimes it didn't feel like I knew what I was doing; but that's how it goes when you are working out your issues, fears, and questions mid- or post-crisis. When you are moving along the path of healing, toward a gold-lacquer-in-the-cracks version of yourself—at times, you have to be willing to go forth not blindly, exactly, but simply, by placing one foot in front of the other.

Once I had stopped seeing Normina, I had to check in more often with myself too. Can I still cry at the stoplight when I need to cry at the stoplight? Sure. Can I still ask my mom for help, but make sure she isn't overdoing it? Yes. For somebody like me, or rather, for *the somebody that was me when I met and married Dave*, any of the above actions would have been impossible. In some ways, I was stuck in terms of personal growth when I was with Dave, not because of him, but because I never knew any other way to be. Nothing had ever necessitated me changing. When somebody you love dies, as terrible or as odd as it is to say, you have a chance to remake yourself. You have the opportunity to take a good long look at yourself and to be humbled by the fact that life is short—are you going to make more of it?

⋙₊₊⋘

We don't like to talk about aging and death in this country; we prefer the myths of eternal youth and beauty. Within a month of Dave's death, I had my will done. It's something I firmly encourage everyone to do—but of course, who the hell wants to plan for their own death? How depressing is that? It's so depressing that we laugh when we are told just how much a living will can help the ones we *will* leave behind. We laugh to stave off the cold stark reality of it, the sadness, the fear, the pain and depression.

Death talk burdens us. Depression and sadness should be avoided at all costs. When someone is depressed, we think they should pull up their boot straps and think positive thoughts. When someone is sad, we do our best to cheer them up. Urging people past their sadness is such a knee-jerk response, I found myself doing it recently when Sean's daughter had her heart broken. I found myself asking, "Are you okay?" when clearly, she wasn't. I checked in then, with myself. Why did I want her to be okay so soon? Is it really that unbearable to be around the brokenhearted, when we have all been right there a dozen times for a dozen reasons before?

Crying is not a sign of weakness, people have to let the pain out. Numbing the pain does not work—I know this. Pushing it to the side, becoming a workaholic—nope! Grief and distress in all forms have to be given space and time. What did I say to my stepdaughter after I realized I was denying her her own feelings? "Hey, I'm not going to ask you if you're okay anymore. I hated hearing that after Dave died. Just know that I'm here if you need me, I'm thinking about you, and I'm throwing positive energy at you."

There is no such thing as *forever.* In some cases, there is no such thing as *you'll get over it,* even if we do eventually have to live like we have, on the surface. Your first break up is devastating, as is your tenth. Honor the process the bereaved have to go through. Honor your own process of grieving—own it, write about it!

You might be able to get away with numbing the pain at first, and in a way, I do believe that doing "nothing but business" was the only way I made it through those first awful months. There is so much I don't remember from that time period, and I'm fine with that. But eventually, I knew I needed help, and I went for any and every kind of help that spoke to me—as wacky as it might have sounded, as "non-me" as it seemed.

Filled With Gold

I did Camp Widow eight months after Dave's death, and loved it. A few months after that, I went to a local grief yoga retreat. I was no yogi, but it was a great transformative experience. For three hours, a group of grieving strangers shared a space and a very open understanding: Some mourners had lost spouses, others a parent or a child, others best friends, and others dogs—but we were all in it together. Using bolsters and supports, we held yoga poses for long periods of time. We listened to music. To address our grief even "more directly," we stood and walked while wearing shrouds over our heads. These shrouds were nothing more than blankets, but when we removed them, we removed our "veils of mourning." I, for one, did feel lighter. I, for one, continued to ask myself, "Will trying this help, will trying that help? Maybe? Okay, I'm going for it!"

If people wondered if I was going off the deep end, it didn't matter. Sometimes I shared what I was doing, sometimes I didn't. Sometimes I engaged in group grieving rituals; other times I read books and processed things completely on my own. What I did do no matter what is this: I did what I wanted.

I wanted to feel better. I could not dwell. For the boys, for myself, for my living friends and family, and for Dave—I had to do whatever it took. I asked the universe to throw in my path all the small and big tools and people that would carry me and my boys forward. I did not judge. I tried a little bit of everything:

- Body Talk healing sessions
- Manifest True Love group
- Reiki classes

169

- Pilates class
- Tap dancing class
- Finding Your Voice singing class
- Mindfulness instruction
- Group meditation

⊶⊷

It's not easy watching a widow grieve. You feel her pain, get a glimpse of the level of pain that lies ahead for you one day, and sometimes, relive what you have already been through. When my mother came to us on Mt. Emily and stayed with us in Union for a whole month, she was probably in as much shock and denial as I was. She was in "survival mode" too, and although her first priority clearly was the boys and me, she was missing Dave too. She was missing my dad.

It can be unbearable to see your child in pain: My mom, like most moms, wanted to fix it—make it go away. She wanted to take care of me, but even knowing grief intimately herself, she couldn't. She knew she couldn't, and that probably made it even tougher. In the beginning, nothing could be said or done to ease the deep ache of losing Dave. My mother began to worry about me a lot more after Dave died—she still does. But as I grew stronger and into my "new Melissa" shoes, I was able to speak up with her in terms of what I needed, and what I did not. I got better with boundaries, and my relationship with my mom has never been better. One day awhile back, my mom and I were walking the Forest Park trails by the Portland Zoo, and I had an epiphany: "Look at us, Mom, two widows on a lovely hike."

Shitty experiences can draw people closer than ever before, and can bring about relationship breakthroughs.

My mother loves Sean. The boys have a great time with him. They know he isn't their father and isn't trying to be. When Bryce overheard Sean talking to me about a conversation he'd had with a work colleague, in which he referred to Bryce as his son—not his stepson—we all felt pretty natural (and warm) about it. Bryce balances out having Dave and Sean and I don't think he feels any guilt over it—I hope he doesn't.

Sean's family embraced us all from Day One. All the little cousins love Brad and Bryce, and our moms hang out together. Sean and I talked about how tight our families were and how much they meant to us when we first started dating, and we are grateful things fell in place the way they did.

When we visit Dave's sister and her family, we feel welcomed. It's not the easiest visit for me, for obvious reasons, but there will probably always be certain times, occasions, and places where those bittersweet feelings around what we all lost will bubble up. I let them, and so does Sean. He would like to visit Wallowa Lake together—scene of so many Dave, Melissa, Brad, and Bryce summer vacations; but at this point, I'm the one who is hesitating. Dave's ashes are in that lake. Bryce and I were recently planning a trip to Union, just the two of us, but as the date pressed closer, I realized I wasn't ready, and cancelled.

You can move forward and you do move forward—sometimes you create a life you never could have envisioned and you are happy. But the concept of "closure" is one I'm not sure I believe in: I'm not sure it's possible, nor the healthiest goal. I will never "be over" Dave's death, and though I accept it now, I wouldn't say I've gained closure on it. I would say I'm not actively grieving anymore. I do visit some of our old haunts without hesitancy, but others, I may never return to—not because I fear breaking down and having to begin at Square One again, I guess you could say, if there is any closure to my grief, it is that I'll never be at Square One, over Dave's death, ever again. Why might I never make it back to the one lake in Eastern Oregon where we spent so much of our time as a family? I don't know. There's just that too: Not knowing.

⟨⟩

In my first year or so of widowhood, one cliché bugged me the most. I was fortunate that nobody ever really said to me, but other widows who had experienced what I had—the sudden death of a loved one—said they'd heard it: "Oh, he went quickly. He didn't suffer, that's better!"

Is it better to die suddenly rather than over many long months or years? I don't know. In my mind, neither way is better, because you know, *someone is dead.* You'll never speak to them or laugh with them or hold their hand again.

If you haven't been on the receiving end of grief yet, if you haven't heard some of the odd things people think or say or try not to say regarding life and death, rest assured: You will. You will lose someone close to you, it's inevitable. If you've had your share of grief and have been lulled into believing an unfair or untimely death cannot possibly happen again in your lifetime, it can. I force myself to recognize this fact—and at the same time to somehow hush the begging me, "Please, universe, not again, what are the odds," and "Please, everyone I love, don't ever stop breathing."

It's challenging to be graceful in the face of the fact of death: The most truthful cliché of all about death is that life is short. I toss this cliché around like candy, even if it isn't always the kind of candy people want, and I apply it to myself on a regular basis. When I'm ruminating about a decision—"Hmmm, but what about ten years from now?"—I stop and think, "Ten years? Ha! I could be gone tomorrow. The world could change in five."

Life is short brings me back to myself and reminds me not to waste so much energy pretending—because that's what we all do—that we can control a single thing.

You are alive today, so if you are unhappy, figure a way through or up or out. You need to live right now: live live live. Now. Don't wait to live until your kids are grown up and out of the house. Don't be afraid to leap into the unknown. Does walking around a yoga studio with a blanket on your head sound intriguing to you? Helpful? Fun or funny? Go for it. Do you want to take a coding class? Go for it. Learn how to tango? Portland is a great city for dance lessons. Follow Cheryl Strayed's route and walk in the wild. Do you! Let go and let be!

I am throwing around these tidbits of what sounds like advice right now just as much for myself as for anybody. I am still a work-in-progress, a cracked vessel that still has a lot more light to let in. There is no closure, no forever, no guarantees, and no beating death. If we know life is short, why is it so hard to take those first steps toward making it better? Yes, the unknown is freaky. Yes, you have to let go of knowing and controlling and fixing. Yes, maybe you just have to say "yes" more often.

Looking back now, I can see I was partially paralyzed before Dave died: I was letting life happen to me. I recognize now when I need to make a move or create movement around me. And I do. If Dave hadn't died, I would not be where I am now. I loved him wholeheartedly while he was alive and with me and together we created a beautiful family; but his death was a catalyst in so many ways. When I first found Normina, she told me: "You can't see it now, but if you do this work, you are going to be a different person."

She was right, and I am grateful for what life and death has brought me.

CHAPTER ELEVEN

Talking about death makes most people uncomfortable—I'm not the first person to have established that. But add to this grim and disturbing topic the act of the dying spouse or partner "choosing" a "next" partner for the one they'll leave behind, and you might witness real repulsion—a visceral reaction. Jaws drop.

"When Mary was dying," someone will say, "she told her husband of forty years, Don, that she wanted him to continue on happily. Part of the happiness Mary imagined for Don entailed him partnering up with her best friend of forty-five years, Linda. Weird, huh? I don't know if I could do that—be so... generous—but oh my God, it worked! Don and Linda even got married!"

When I visited the psychic and she told me Dave was present, I felt an indescribable surge of emotions. I'm sure a word exists for this flash flood of excitement, wonder, sadness, longing, warmth, draining, desperation, and comfort—probably in German, right? But in English, well, whatever was happening in that psychic's office space that day, part of it was just too stunning. Although of course I had gone to her with high hopes Dave would "show," I'd been totally unprepared to hear that he had picked someone else for me to meet and be happy with.

"He assures you too, Melissa, he wants this for you—he wants you to be happy."

Yes, Dave manifesting for me that day was exactly what I'd wanted, but I had to pocket the "there's another guy for you" stuff for a later date. Meet another man? *And do what?* Date him? Hold his hand? Tell him our story? Introduce the boys to him? *And feel what?* Like him? Want him? Love him? Eh, no. Not possible.

Dave and I had never talked about such a thing—*If you and I don't work out and decide to go our separate ways...* Nope! We simply took it for granted we would be together until death did us part, and on that matter, we weren't even comfortable creating our wills. Without really being aware of it, we believed death would *not* part us until we were withered and wrinkled and shuffling around town with walkers. We figured, like most couples, we would have time to deal with "death prep" once we started to *feel* old. Maybe we'd get serious after one of us had a malignant mole removed, or got dentures.

That's how we are supposed to roll—I know financial planners and attorneys who go on and on at barbecues and pool parties about how careless 99% of the American population is: "We're all going to die and we know it, but nobody wants to take a few hours out of their life to deal with this fact. As if ignoring death will keep it at bay or make it go away. As if those who are left behind won't fight and bicker and waste thousands more dollars trying to settle an estate."

Someone dies and we're left with all our "what ifs," but look at how masterful we are at living "as if" we were immortal.

Hundreds of books are written on this topic—write a living will, work up an estate plan, be prepared, and stop living as if you and yours are special snowflakes that will be gifted with Forever. These books are chock full of wise words and they sell like hotcakes, but you wouldn't know it. So I'll take a moment to pass along one other helpful tip in this book: If you haven't done so already, make an appointment this month to plan for your death, and then encourage everyone you know to do the same. Talking more realistically and openly about death won't make it easier or more pleasant, but it can't make things worse.

⊱⊰

Loving again after Dave's death was very scary and confusing. The journal notes I kept when Sean and I first started dating are saturated with undertones—and overtones and just plain tones—of "Oh no, I think we're getting too close. Oh no, I might get hurt."

Actually, I know now that it was a scary and confusing time for both of us. Sean, always the information collector, told me he did a lot of Googling on "How to date a widow." He didn't want to say or do the wrong thing. He wanted to steer clear of "off topics." He didn't want to pry. He didn't see me as fragile, but he didn't want to risk making me sad.

For me, feeling safe was key. Of course, my safety switch after Dave's death might have worked more like a hair trigger. While falling for Sean (hey, falling in love is itself illogical), I kept bouncing back to the highly illogical thought (obsession): "But wait, I never want to hurt again and love has proven hurtful, so I better stop this relationship."

My fears manifested in rejection. I'd more or less stopped obsessing over the boys dying suddenly in their sleep, but whenever the smallest thing with Sean went wrong, I'd feel slighted. I'd pull away: "I'm done! There you go!" Of course, this self-protective defense was normal—widowed or not, male or female, we all carry this instinct to some degree. We all carry the normal dater's angst of, "Gah, what if so-and-so sees all of me? What if he doesn't fully love me like this other guy did?"

To top it off, the "all of me" was new to me too! Passing the year-and-a-half mark without Dave, I was opening up a fresh new Melissa and testing her out. Sean was the first person I was fully exposing her to.

By the time I decided to start dating, eighteen or nineteen months after Dave's death, I wasn't actively grieving. Sure, it had been fifteen-plus years after the last time I'd dated—and I was wearing braces!!!—but I was moving forward. I was going to school and feeling great about it. I had done lots of work on myself. Grief still came to me sporadically, but it was short-lived. Deep pain was replaced by occasional moments of sadness and longing.

Dating Sean was fun. Those journal entries contain fearful tones, but I was excited too. We went to restaurants and concerts, took long walks, and talked and laughed a lot.

I'd returned to my city of Portland and was returning to life there. *Things were beginning to look possible.*

Sean and I definitely did some of the back and forth dance new couples do, and it took about a year to get our shit together, but tentativeness eventually began to give way to trust. When the first hints things might be getting serious popped up, yes, I worried: *Is this too soon? Am I moving at a decent and respectable widow's pace?*

But then I caught myself: *I have moved past caring what others think.* I had done my reading and my reaching out for help and my work—I knew there was no such thing as a widow's "correct timeline." I'd removed my wedding ring when it felt right to me, hadn't I? I'd tried all sorts of therapies—"standard" and "alternative." I'd seen a psychic (two, actually).

Well then, I was going to go for it! Sean and I were comfortable together, so what did I need him to know? How did I talk to him about Dave now? How much should I tell him?

Dating is tough. Dating over the age of forty is somewhat tougher. Dating after being widowed in your forties—seriously?

But Sean—again, as an information collector—made it easy for me. He had done his "how to date a widow" homework, and had read the widow literature: *This is who you are, and this is what happened. Talk to your partner about it.* Neither of us had the intention of getting as deep as we did as quickly as we did. I certainly thought I would raise my kids and get them on their way, and then focus again on my life and maybe on finding a partner. But there was no denying what

Sean and I were both trying—each in our own way—to deny: We could build a wonderful life together.

I did talk to Sean about Dave, and he was generous and balanced with his questions and responses. He proved to be an incredible listener. This is so important, or at least it was to me. It has been important to me too, Sean's support, in writing this book. He knows I would have done it no matter what, because this is my truth and this is my story and I hope it reaches the people it needs to reach. Sean knows whereas I used to be the Melissa who sometimes "lost herself" to her partner—yes, to Dave—I am now *this* Melissa—the one he fell in love with and married and blended families with.

He knows I'm the Melissa who still dreads Christmas. This is hard: Sean and his entire family love Christmas. His father is the person who buys every single person on his list the most perfect present imaginable. Sean's father, like Sean, listens—he listens year-round and when you pull one of his gifts to you from under the tree, you know he's hit the nail on the head.

But December 9th marks Dave's and my wedding anniversary. Then comes Christmas and all the pain associated with that first holiday without him. A few weeks later marks the anniversary of Dave's death.

How that works—how you can have decades straight of awesome Christmases but then one comes along and obliterates them all—I don't know. I'm still anti-winter. Dave's birthday is in February. The boys and I wrote our notes and placed them in those balloons and the day was frigid. The balloons floated almost hesitantly up into a clear blue sky. So, yes, please, somebody cut that three-month period from all calendars and let's call it a day.

Sean has all these dates marked on his Google calendar. I discovered this accidentally, but it only shows how much care he takes in keeping Dave's memory alive. Sean goes all out for Christmas, and I don't want him to change. Maybe one year, I'll be almost as wild for the smell of pine needles, the wrapping of the presents, and the glow of the lights as he is. Maybe one day, that first Christmas without Dave when I had to put the lights up myself and could barely freaking stand it, will be a dim memory.

Either way, I am safe with Sean. He admits he'll never understand why the past few awesome Christmases our families have shared don't add up and smudge out the blues of winter for me. Even in other seasons, he'll notice that after a particularly trying time with the boys, I'll "check out." I know it's hard for Sean, and these are the moments he'll say straight out: "It feels like there are two of us here—two husbands."

And I'll say: "Yes, right now I'm missing Dave. Sometimes I miss his influence."

But Sean and I, as a couple, have adapted to these moments of duality. Love doesn't go away, not in my heart and mind anyway. I had a long relationship with Dave and most of the pages in this book are written about him. That said, Sean is who I'm with now, and I'm so grateful for this chapter of my life.

⊶┼┼⊷

Years ago at Camp Widow, I met Cassie. Her deceased husband had also been a teacher named Dave. In 2012, Cassie wrote about the awkward, scary, funky, but totally hopeful and inspired times her potential future new partner could look forward to. You can see why she and I bonded:

"... I have hope that I will love again... I think about the things I want to say to that person who's out there, waiting for me... I want to say... Don't give up hope. I'm here, waiting. I have so much love to give and now truly understand how love is really all we have. Those moments of joy experienced with our loved ones make the inevitable loss of life more bearable. I will be more centered, present, and appreciative in our relationship than if I hadn't been widowed. It's not a liability. It's a gift to you."

In widowspeak, we talk about Chapter Two. Michelle Steinke-Baumgard, aka, One Fit Widow, gave her Chapter Two, Keith Baumgard, a guest spot on her blog (he has his own blog, Mending While Blending). In writing about being Chapter Two, he notes that when he and Michelle first started dating, he wondered if she could or would love him, but that eventually he came to understand it's always possible to love more than one person, and more importantly, that we all love the people we love differently. The Chapter Two label might bother some, or be a bit too reductive—I can see that—but for people who date widows or widowers, having a supportive community to turn to is important. You will not always be able to anticipate our feelings or "save us from them." Something might set us off on a crying jag or cause us to "check out" briefly; but trust that it will have nothing to do with you, it will be grief—and grief, like love, never dies.

⭠┼┼⭢

Sean and I could have moved into a yurt, but of course, our kids wouldn't have found that fun or interesting. By the time we began to blend our families, Brad was in Boys Town. I knew he would graduate there, but still, making sure Bryce and Jasmine were okay with the new arrangement was a big deal. Sean and I had talked a lot about parenting and knew our styles differed. We decided it was important to stay clear that Brad and Bryce had a dad—Dave—and Sean wouldn't take his place. Likewise, Jasmine had a mom I would never replace.

Early on, we established a few base "rules:" we eat dinner as a whole family together, no matter what, several times a week, and we hold bi weekly family meetings. We don't always make our own rules stick—we're human after all—but we do a good job. We aren't the Brady Bunch, but who is? Heck, I don't think the Brady Bunch should be held up as a role model—there wasn't any mention ever of either deceased spouse, and that's not healthy!

Communicating is the most challenging piece we have had in regards to blending families, but we all knew going into it that harmony and flow wouldn't occur overnight. Talking about what's working and what isn't working helps. And respect is key—we're fortunate, I think, that our kids manage to keep respect on display in most situations.

I feel like I've lived two lives, and honestly, both lives have been amazing. I've had my constants—my family, the boys, and my friends—but I have changed. Probably if you asked a friend, "Has Melissa changed since Dave's death?" they'd say, "No. I don't notice much of a difference. She's always been smart, strong, and goofy."

But besides feeling slightly more cynical than I used to be—sorry, not sorry!—I know that who I am now would not work with Dave, and who I was then would not work with Sean. Dave was the perfect partner for who I was then; Sean is the perfect partner for who I am now.

⚔

When I was at Camp Widow, though no one ever said this directly to me, I heard about the ongoing "debate" about which is worse: losing a spouse through death or through divorce. *Wait—what?* Yes, some people actually have said to widows: "You're so lucky your husband died, because you don't have to deal with him ever again."

Granted, some divorces are completely traumatic, and I don't deny anyone their feelings of loss and devastation, but the death/divorce comparison feels like apples and oranges to me. It also feels beyond super insensitive to insist that widows *have it better*: Divorce is a choice (for at least one person in the partnership); but death is not a choice—someone is simply ripped away from you.

I've asked a few times throughout this book why it seems humans require tragedy or trauma to jolt them toward a better understanding of themselves and of what it means to be human. When Dave was torn from our lives, at first I was numb, and then I was raw—as raw as an open wound. Any masks I'd been wearing, subconsciously or not, fell away and shattered. From the ashes—pardon the cliché—I rebuilt, and evolved somehow into a truer version of the person I was meant to be. I emerged from deep *deep* pain, more whole.

I wish Dave didn't have to die for this to have happened—obviously. And nobody will ever know what else might have triggered me to really dig in—heart, mind, and soul—and grow. All I do know is that I had to get past the pain for Brad and Bryce, and that doing so involved trying anything and everything that seemed like it might help. Because I held so much of the trauma of losing Dave in my body, I did a ton of body work. I did yoga, pilates, tap dancing, and BodyTalk sessions; I got massages, and even pedicures were self care.

I won't know where widowed readers of this book are—how far out—and I know that at first, it's possible that nothing will seem like it could possibly help. *Pilates and pedicures—are you kidding? I'm freaking depressed.* I know you'll want to pull the covers over your head and hide. But wherever you are in your grieving process, the best words I can offer are: Go easy on yourself. Don't be too hard on yourself. Don't watch the news, because the bad stories will add to the weight you are carrying on your chest, and any happy stories that *do* manage to make it to mainstream media, will only make you cry harder. Take family and friends up on as many of their offerings as you can—let them take you shopping, let them take you out of the house—but also know that it's okay sometimes to say, "No, thank you," turn out the lights, and cry alone into a pillow.

I may always be anti-snow, probably because of everything that happened in that house on Mt. Emily. I have no desire to play in the snow ever again. Sean has talked about taking time off and renting a mountain cabin, but as of now, I want no part of it. Normally I'm an accommodating person, I'll do anything, but just thinking about snow and ice and remoteness makes me feel trapped and takes me right back to that other chapter of my life.

This is me, doing the best I can—still. This is me keeping the lines of communication as open as possible. This is me being thankful for the support I've had before Dave died, and ever since. I don't trust in forever and never will, but I do trust myself. There is no right or wrong way through grief and there is no closure. I think the best we can do is to get to a place where we honor what our truest core and body are saying: You, me, the person sitting to your right or left—none of us has any control over anything. The world as we know it can turn upside down in a flash. But we can control how we respond. We can get to the place where we love ourselves, and from there, can rest a bit easier in knowing that we will be okay.

ABOUT THE AUTHOR

Melissa Grahek Pierce went through a tremendous trial when she lost her husband. Now, she helps other widows cope with their own losses and move forward. She enjoys her roles as a wife, mother, sister, life coach, and friend. Melissa currently calls Portland, Oregon, home. She can be reached through her website www.filledwithgold.org

Christine Fadden helped Melissa put her thoughts and feelings down on the page. Fadden graduated from the Warren Wilson MFA Program for Writers. She has been published in the *Museum of Americana, More Than Sports Talk, Germ Magazine,* the *American Literary Review,* and *Hobart* magazine. She won the 2014 Tennessee Williams Fiction Prize and was a finalist for the *Cobalt Review* 2016 Earl Weaver Baseball Writing Prize.